LIVE LIKE YOU BELIEVE

10 Power Moves To Heal. Rise. Lead.

LIVE LIKE YOU BELIEVE

10 Power Moves To
Heal. Rise. Lead.

LORETTA MCNARY

Copyright © 2025, Live Like You Believe, Loretta McNary

ALL RIGHTS RESERVED.
No part of this publication may be reproduced, stored in a retrieval system, or transmitted in any form or by any means—electronic, mechanical, photocopying, recording, or otherwise—without the prior written permission of the publisher, except in the case of brief quotations used in reviews or articles.

Live Like You Believe: 10 Power Moves to Heal. Rise. Lead.
ISBN: 978-0-9841096-2-3

First Edition: 2025

Cover and interior design by [Five Seven Media]
Printed in the United States of America

Edited and formatted by
sheliawritesbooks@yahoo.com
www.sheliawritesbooks.com

Published by
Five Seven Media
Southaven, MS

www.LiveLikeYouBelieve.net

Scripture quotations, unless otherwise noted, are taken from the Holy Bible, New International Version® (NIV®). Copyright ©1973, 1978, 1984, 2011 by Biblica, Inc.® Used by permission. All rights reserved worldwide.

This book is a work of nonfiction and reflects the author's personal experiences, beliefs, and interpretations. Names and identifying details may have been changed to protect privacy.

For more resources, gatherings, and community inspiration, visit:
www.LiveLikeYouBelieve.net

Table of Contents

Dedication ii
Acknowledgements iii
Introduction iii
Power Move #1: Heal Like You Believe 1
Power Move #2: Lead Like You Believe 17
Power Move #3: Walk Like You Believe 25
Power Move #4: Reach Like You Believe 36
Power Move #5: Receive Like You Believe 46
Power Move #6: Trust Like You Believe 56
Power Move #7: Forgive Like You Believe 64
Power Move #8: Give Like You Believe 73
Power Move #9: Rise Like You Believe 80
Power Move #10: Pray Like You Believe 92
The Final Page—Never the End 104
About Loretta 107
Other Books by Loretta 108
Connect with Loretta 109

Dedication

First and always, to God. Thank you for entrusting me with this sacred assignment to call others back to belief. Belief in Your promises. Belief in their healing. Belief in joy after sorrow, purpose after pain, and wholeness after what tried to break them. Thank You for carrying me through the crushing so that I could write from a place of truth, grace, and glory, not just theory. You didn't just give me words; You gave me wisdom. Thank You for never letting go.

To my five extraordinary sons: Brandon, Marshall, Nicholas, Spencer, and Jacob; You all are my heartbeat, my reason, my reward, and my legacy.

Brandon (Resting in Power), your strength, your courage, and your light live in me forever. I will carry your love and compassion with me every day I live.

Marshall, your steady faith and quiet power remind me that peace is a strength.

Nicholas, your drive and brilliance push me to keep rising and creating.

Spencer, your insight and presence show me the power of perspective and purpose.

Jacob, your love for adventure and family inspires me to enjoy my life unapologetically.

ACKNOWLEDGEMENTS

To Tiara, Anitra, Kylin, and Naomi, just being in my life brings me love and joy.

To my parents:
Dad, Dave Shorter Jr. (Resting in Power), thank you for modeling the value of family first. Thank you for teaching me the value of integrity and the importance of a strong work ethic.

Mom, Dorothy Shorter-Peggs, thank you for showing me grace, order, and the quiet strength of a Mother.

To my family: Thank you for your prayers, your encouragement, and your love.

To my faithful friends: Thank you for standing in the gap; you helped hold up my arms when they felt too tired to lift.

And to you, Dear Reader: This book is for you—the person silently unraveling while holding it all together. The one who has almost given up on becoming. The one who refuses to pretend and is ready to rise and lead. Come back to these pages whenever you need truth, courage, or clarity.

With love and purpose,
Loretta McNary

> *"You are not too late. You are not too broken. You are not too much. You are becoming exactly as God intended. Live healed. Live whole. Live like you believe."*
>
> — LORETTA MCNARY

Introduction

There was a time I wore strength like armor, smiling on stages, showing up for everyone, and producing inspiration like clockwork even while I was falling apart inside. I didn't realize it then, but I was performing strength, not living from it. I thought if I could keep going, keep achieving, keep pretending, maybe the *ache* would quiet itself. But silence does not necessarily mean healing. And I was carrying pain that had learned how to *dress itself up* in excellence and achievement.

It took several seasons of *breaking* for me to finally see what I had been avoiding—a divine interruption. A painful pause. A hard stop that I didn't choose but desperately needed.

That season in 2023, God didn't ask me to do more; He asked me to sit with what was already broken. When I obeyed Him, I met myself, the real me. The unmasked, unedited, but still loved version of me. The one I had been burying under performance, politeness, and the pressure to be everything for everyone.

This book was born in that place. Not on the mountaintop of victory, but in the valley where faith becomes real, where healing is messy, and where rising doesn't look like soaring, it looks like crawling until your knees become strong enough to walk again.

"Live Like You Believe" is a lifeline. It is what God whispered to me when I had nothing left but breath and the tiniest trace of hope. It's what pulled me out of despair and reminded me that belief is more than words; it's action. It's showing up with tears in your eyes and saying, "I am still here". It's trusting that Heaven is not just watching, but backing your every step, even the fearful ones.

In these pages, I'll take you with me, through the fear, the falls, the unlearning, and the sacred rebuilding. You will not be asked to be perfect here. You will not be asked to hide your hurt. But you *will* be challenged to live fully. To stop playing small. To stop apologizing for the fire in your bones.

Live Like You Believe is about power, but not the world's kind. This is the power that comes from healing while in the process of becoming. It's permission to live in your truth. It's permission to start walking away from what broke you and running straight toward what blesses you. This is about the power of *becoming*, not someone new, but someone *true*.

You'll read about pain, yes, but also joy that can't be shaken. You'll be reminded that survival is not your standard; excellence is. You were called to heal, to *rise and to lead*. You'll learn how to stop performing for love and instead receive it. Not just from others but from God, and from the you that's been buried beneath years of fear and false peace.

So let me tell you plainly, what you hold in your hands carries weight. Not the weight that burdens, but the kind that anchors you in truth and awakens what the world tried to lull to sleep. These pages are soaked with sacred fire, lived experience, and the kind of revelation that doesn't leave you the same. Every chapter is a gentle uncovering and a divine confrontation. You will be seen here, not just as you've been but as you're becoming.

And as you read, something will begin to stir. Not all at once. Not with lightning and thunder. But quietly, deeply, like roots remembering they were meant to reach, like a heart learning how to beat for something eternal again. You may cry in these pages. You may pause. You may return to a line that feels like it was written for you alone. That's the point. My prayer is that you are not just reading, but your soul is remembering.

There's a version of you that's not waiting to be created; it's waiting to be revealed, and she's been so patient. She's been whispering under the noise, the obligations, and the expectations that were never yours to carry. She is not the woman who fakes "I'm fine", who trades her voice for validation, who shrinks to keep the peace. She is bold. She is wise. She is kind. She is full of heaven's authority and earth's assignment. It is time to come back for her.

By the time you finish this book, my deepest prayer is that you will no longer seek permission to heal, to rise, to speak, to lead, or to believe. Instead, you will do it. Somewhere along the way, you will remember what has always been true: you were called to *Live Like You Believe*. You were designed for this. You were being prepared, even in the crushing. And when you show up fully, so does the life that's been waiting, not for your perfection, but for your presence.

So, turn the pages, beloved. There's so much more ahead. AND, it looks a lot like the best version of you.

Loretta McNary

Power Move 1
Heal Like You Believe

"I tell you, you can pray for anything, and if you believe that you've received it, it will be yours." Mark 11:24 (NLT)

The truth is, I had fallen before. A few months before the day that everything changed, I had taken a tumble in the church parking lot. It was after service, the kind of cool yet sunny Sunday morning where you feel God in the breeze and believe the week ahead will be full of open doors and good news. I wasn't running, nor was I rushing; I was just walking to my car, heels clicking against the concrete like always. This time, I accidentally stepped into a crack, the kind you don't see until you're down on the ground. I hit my knees hard. They scraped, bled a little, and bruised a lot. Yet, it wasn't the blood that stung; it was my pride.

Although I was between two cars when I fell, a couple walking to their car noticed me on the ground, came over, and asked if they could help. I said no and tried to get up on my own, but I couldn't. They reached down and lifted me up. I thanked them, and they asked if they could help me with my car. Again, I replied, "No, but thank you so much for asking," as I limped quietly to my car.

That fall hurt my ego more than my knees. I tried to hold back the tears so I could call my sons to let them know I had fallen. I tried to play it off, and they each asked if I needed anything. I assured them that I was good.

I drove home in silence. I didn't tell anyone else about my fall, because it felt like a fluke, a flinch in time, something I could cover with a band-aid and keep moving. However, I carried it with me in my mind. The ache in my knees. The sting in my dignity. There was also a tiny whisper I didn't want to hear: *slow down.* To be honest, I had heard the whisper many times over the past few years. I didn't listen. Ninety days later, the mental band-aids weren't enough anymore.

I will never ever forget Sunday, March 5, 2023. The day started like an answered prayer. The kind of day where the sun doesn't just shine—it sings. The message at church had been a personal love letter from heaven, echoing in my spirit like a promise sealed in fire: "Be strong and courageous, for the Lord your God is with you wherever you go." I walked out wearing that scripture like armor, like perfume. I was strong. I was courageous. I was seen. I was ready for a great day!

Until I fell. Yes, I fell while walking. Not metaphorically, not symbolically, but physically, I hit the ground. I had the bone-snapping, breath-stealing, world-shaking kind of fall.

One moment, I was walking back to my car to grab my sunglasses before heading to brunch with a new client, and the next, I was collapsed on the pavement, my leg twisted unnaturally, bones broken, nerves screaming, skin barely holding everything together.

From my point of view, it looked like a regular sidewalk. You take calculated steps until you reach a simple curb, and then you take a single step. I slowed my steps as I got near the curb, but it was a hidden two-step, staggered curb, and I had no idea such a thing even existed. I saw the top curb in front of me, so I moved forward with confidence. What I didn't see was the second step below it. That invisible drop changed everything. My foot slipped on that unseen step, and in a single breath, my entire world shattered.

It was not a graceful stumble. Nor was it a quick *catch-yourself before you tumble*. It felt like I was flying through the air in slow motion. The fall was hard. I fell wrong. I fell into the kind of pain that rewrites your understanding of the definition of unrelenting pain.

My body hit the pavement like glass. My leg collapsed beneath me, bones shifting into places they were never meant to go. I couldn't move. Couldn't scream. For a moment, I didn't know if I was even breathing. I looked down and saw my right leg twisted, unnaturally bent. The pain wasn't just physical. When I finally realized what had happened and looked down at my leg again, I was shocked to see my right leg disfigured. The bones seemed to be trying to break through my skin. I panicked. I cried out in pain.

My client walked over to me and asked, "Are you okay?" Then she looked down at my leg. She said, "Oh no, we have to get you to the hospital."

In that moment, I was no longer Loretta McNary, the mother who believes in miracles, the woman who always finds a way, the fixer, the fierce one, the glue. I was Loretta—the broken woman, lying in the street, unable to move.

It was the next move I knew I had to make that stole my breath. I had to call my sons. If only I could find a way not to tell them, but the call was inevitable, I had to utter the words no mother ever wanted to say, "I'm hurt." My voice was so small. Shaking. Strangled with sobs I didn't see coming.

"Hey, son, I fell," I whispered. "I broke my leg. I... I can't move. The fall was so hard, my Apple Watch called 911. The paramedics are on the way."

At that moment, I shattered—not from the fall, but from the humbleness of being seen broken. And with every syllable, my heart was broken into jagged little pieces because I knew they would see me like. Hurting. Helpless. Human. And they would feel the same. Hurt. Helpless. Human.

That was the moment I will never forget. Not when I hit the pavement. Not when my bones buckled. But when I realized my sons would see me not as the unshakable matriarch, but as a woman in pain, and not just physical pain.

I was dealing with spiritual pain, too. I had convinced myself that as long as I kept "serving," "showing up," and "smiling," then life would reward me with immunity from suffering.

One thing I needed to learn was that sometimes the greatest act of faith is not standing tall, but letting the people who love you *see you when you fall. I also needed to see myself in a different light.*

I saw a woman who encouraged everyone else while quietly ignoring the screams of her own soul. I saw a woman wearing strength like armor but hiding battle wounds no one knew she had, nor did anyone ever ask her if she was really okay. I often wondered if anyone would ever take the time to look deep enough and long enough to see that I was not okay.

I saw a woman addicted to performing wholeness, terrified to admit she was sometimes mentally bruised, and yet continued to show up for others even under the stage lights, while spiritually broken.

The paramedics arrived quickly. But when they examined me, their concern intensified. The pulse was faint—barely there in my right foot. What I did not know at the time was that my blood flow was compromised, and time was now a factor. I was unable to go to my preferred hospital. They had to rush me to the nearest hospital without delay.

Heal Like You Believe

Upon arrival and a brief intake, I was instantly admitted. The surgery was scheduled for a few days after my fall. It lasted for hours, but it was successful.

Titanium now lives inside of me—a rod that replaced the broken bone in my leg, a plate to hold my ankle together, and more screws than I can count, each one a tiny symbol of survival, holding fragments in place that once felt irreparable.

The other bone was fractured too, but with it came hope. The surgeon explained that it might still fuse together over time. That word "*might* "landed like a prayer and a dare all at once.

I was released from the hospital the next evening after comprehensive surgery. However, not to my life as it was, but to a new reality I hadn't been prepared for: a walker, a mountain of prescriptions, a bedpan chair, medical debt, and strict orders not to place a single ounce of weight on my right leg for months. It felt like being handed a body I didn't recognize, a life I didn't ask for, and a silence I didn't know how to fill. I was also unable to drive for almost a year.

My new way of walking involved holding onto the walker and using my left leg to hop. Yes, hop, hop, and hop.

Once I was finally at home, my soul began to tremble. I felt myself slipping into despair. There were days when I couldn't fake it. I couldn't encourage myself. I could no longer wear strength like a crown. Everything changed. My bedroom became my world. My movement, once effortless, now required coordination and courage. The smallest things—brushing my teeth, bathing, getting dressed, hoping to the other side of the room—became complicated rituals marked by pain, pride, and a constant awareness that my life had been forever altered.

My faith began to shake under the weight of it all. I felt myself slipping into despair, inch by inch, prayer by unanswered prayer. I was down; not just physically, but emotionally, spiritually, and mentally.

Still... I showed up. I showed up because my son showed up every day for me. He prepared three meals a day for me and placed them on my tray in my bedroom day after day for months.

The Woman on the Screen and the One Behind the Curtain

A few times a week, despite it all, I hosted my television show from my living room. I would use the walker and hop into the room, placing my walker discreetly out of camera view. I would then sit upright in the carefully arranged chair and press the button that brought the lights to life. The camera would come on, and so would I.

People saw the polished version. They heard the voice that still had power. They saw the woman with purpose and poise, still curating conversations and spreading joy.

What they didn't see was the moment the show ended, how I would exhale slowly, painfully, and shift my mind back to a reality that held no glamour, no ease, and no soft place to land. I would sit in silence, in pain from the effort, blinking away tears that had been carefully timed to only fall after the last goodbye was said on-air.

Behind the scenes, I was breaking and rebuilding at the same time. I was in the most vulnerable place I had ever been. Behind the scenes, I was learning to *be with God in my suffering, not just my success.*

There were days and weeks when I would do nothing but cry and pray, and cry some more. I felt like the original version of me was barely living, and that all of my dreams were dying with it.

At the time, I was serving as a deaconess in my church. Each week, I received emailed prayer requests.

Praying for others became the oxygen I needed. Eventually, I created a prayer board in my closet. While praying for others, I decided to include my own prayers, as well as those of my family and friends, on the prayer board.

Looking back, I realize that was the beginning of my healing. There were still months of physical therapy ahead, countless follow-up visits to my orthopedic surgeon, and I still had fear and doubt that I was dealing with each day.

One day, I realized I was beginning to trust the healing process, both physically and spiritually. I was not crying as much. I was beginning to trust God's timing. I was beginning to trust myself again.

I had no idea "Live Like You Believe" was being birthed during that very season. In the wreckage. In the silence. In the stillness. Not in spite of the pain, but because of it.

When Crying Becomes Prayer and Prayer Becomes Air

I didn't know prayer could sound like weeping. I didn't know God could be so close to the sobs that had no words. I didn't know that healing could begin with a declaration, and in a *desperation* so raw it made healthy bones shake.

Eventually, my prayer board and my prayer closet both became my little sanctuary of scribbled hopes and whispered needs. I didn't just go there to be spiritual—I went there to survive. Until one day, when the tears ran dry and my chest felt empty, I did something I hadn't done in years. I literally cried out loud, not elegantly, not with crafted language, but with a soul-wide scream: "Lord God almighty, please have mercy... I need to feel Your presence."

Right there, in the middle of my nothingness, and within the darkness of my prayer closet, God whispered something I will never forget: *"The struggle is only in your mind."*

It was like peace slid into the room through the crack under the door. Nothing changed on the outside in that moment, but something shifted in me. A stillness that didn't erase the pain but sat right there with it. A kindness that didn't fix the problem but held me close like a promise. That was the starting point of *my* healing. Not just the surface kind, but the kind that starts restoring the woman inside.

When Confidence Returns Without Applause

There were still months of physical therapy ahead. Countless follow-up visits with my orthopedic surgeon. Many more tears. Then somewhere along the journey, the edge of my sadness began to dull. The heaviness started to lift, until six months later, when I was awakened from my sleep by intense pain in my right side. Again, I was rushed to the ER.

I was told I had a kidney stone, which required surgery to remove. Here we go again. Shock. Pain. Disbelief. After surgery, I cried out again, and again, "Lord God, I need your help, this is too much."

This time, my answer was found days later when I felt surrounded by a profound peace so strong it covered my entire world. It was like I was drowning, but once I stopped struggling, I could feel a sense of calmness. I remembered what I knew to be true, stopped fighting the process, stood up, and focused my attention on my breathing. One breath at a time.

While recovering from kidney stone surgery, I realized I needed to trust God's process and *God's* timing. Not because I needed to return to who I was prior to the fall, but because I had discovered and accepted a deeper, truer version of myself in the stillness. The version I had long buried beneath busyness, expectations, and performance.

Restoration isn't about going back to old ways of life, but about becoming a better version of who we were created to be. It is about becoming whole from the inside out. It is about remembering to *live like you believe*. Things will continue to happen that we cannot control, but our job is to trust God.

Reflection: The Truth Beneath the Bandages

Most of us have been taught to call it *strength* when we smile through pain. We learned to applaud survival as if it were the highest prize we could win. We have memorized scriptures, pushed through meetings, and served until our bodies whispered warnings that we refused to hear. However, there comes a moment, an unshakeable, holy moment, when pretending becomes too expensive. When the weight of performing wholeness becomes too heavy to carry. When the quiet ache we buried years ago begins to swell in our chest, demanding to be acknowledged, not silenced. That moment doesn't always arrive with a fall like mine. Sometimes it comes in the middle of the night, when sleep won't stay. Sometimes it comes in a conversation where you suddenly hear yourself talking like a stranger. Sometimes it comes in the mirror when the person looking back at you feels far away.

But it *will* come. And when it does, it will not be your ruin. It will be your revival. Your re-entry. Your return to yourself. To the person who is still struggling. To the child of God who is still worthy of tenderness even in our tears.

I made a much-needed decision. I would no longer pretend. I would no longer perform. Instead, I would heal. Not patch. Not conceal, but deeply, painfully, and beautifully heal. Here's the truth no one told me—*you cannot genuinely heal while you're still wrapped in temporary mental bandages, soaked in fear, shame, and silence.* You have to rip them off even when it stings, especially when it stings.

More Truth Beneath the Bandages

Sometimes I think we've been tricked. I always believed that strength meant never showing weakness. That success meant covering scars with makeup and a smile. That being "okay" was enough to pass as being fulfilled. So, I learned how to walk wounded in cute heels.

I perfected the art of high functioning while my heart was broken. I hid behind my strengths, talent, busyness, and Bible verses I barely believed anymore. I performed. I pretended. Still hurt under designer bandages, hoping no one noticed the limp in my walk or my spirit.

The truth is, God sees us, and He is NOT ashamed of us. He is not looking for our *perfection*. He is looking for *permission* to heal us.

8 Life-Changing Lessons from My Ongoing Recovery:

1. **My pain is honest. I will let it speak, but not control it.** I stopped silencing my ache. Pain doesn't make you weak. Ignoring it does.

2. **Healing begins when hiding ends.** Real power isn't in patching—it is in peeling the bandage back and letting the light in.

3. **God doesn't need our performance. He desires our presence.** I met Him more in my tears than in my titles.

4. **Let people see you when it's not pretty.** My sons didn't love me less in that moment. They loved me deeper.

5. **Brokenness is not failure—it is a doorway to freedom.** My shattered bones were not the end of me. They were the beginning of my becoming.

6. **Stop settling for 'not bad.'** You were not created to cope. You were born to *conquer*.

7. **Your real life starts when the fake one ends.** The bandaged version of you is not the boldest version of you.

8. **Healing doesn't erase the scar—it makes it sacred.** Every scar tells a story of a woman who lived, loved, and refused to give up.

Reflections: Get Your Healing

Heal. Heal for real. Stop pretending that survival is enough. Stop wearing perfection as a mask to hide the pain. Do not apologize any longer for your process, nor minimize your needs. Heal out loud. Rest without guilt. Speak your truth, even if your voice shakes.

Rise—not because I am unbreakable, but because I have finally stopped hiding the places where I was broken. I will live like I believe that God will heal the woman behind the bandage. I live with grace, sisterhood, and fierce faith!

This is your moment to commit to complete healing. I hope that after reading this chapter, which shares a tough moment in my life, you will allow your healing to begin, and that you will stop pretending that *barely getting by* is the same as thriving. I pray you will stop believing that *not bad* is the best life has to offer, and that you will stop performing like the wound isn't real.

I encourage you to rip off the proverbial bandage. Call your healing what it is: holy, hard, necessary. *Live like you believe* you deserve more. *Live like you believe* you are worth the miracles. *Live like you believe* that He still has a plan, because He does. His plan for you is so much bigger than you could ever imagine.

Questions

1. What truth have I quietly buried because I was afraid that acknowledging it would unravel the image I worked so hard to keep together?

_____
_____
_____
_____
_____
_____
_____
_____

2. What version of me have I created to cope, and what would it cost to lay her down and reclaim the real me?

_____
_____
_____
_____
_____
_____
_____
_____

3. Where have I confused survival with healing, and what does it look like to stop numbing and start feeling again?

_____
_____
_____
_____

Journal Prompt: *To the Person I've Been Pretending to Be*

Write a letter to the version of yourself who kept showing up when she was exhausted, who smiled when she was in pain, who carried others while quietly bleeding. Thank her. Honor her. Then, give her permission to live like she believes.

Invite the real you to return—not the perfect one, but the present one. The woman God sees beneath all the bandages. The one who is still brave, still worthy, and still becoming.

Heal Like You Believe

Prayer: *I'm Ready to Heal Without Hiding*

Father God,

I have worn strength like armor and my silence like protection. I have convinced the world—and myself—that I'm fine, even when I am not. But You see what we cannot. You have watched me walk wounded and still call it faith. You have heard the prayers I never said out loud. You know the pain I've tried to cover up instead of surrendering.

Today, I will stop hiding. Today, I will stop performing. Today, I say the words that have been locked in my chest. I need healing. I need You. I need to come home to my original version of who you created me to be. I don't want a life that looks whole but feels less than. I want real peace. Real presence. Real restoration. I trust that You, the God who saw me when I fell, will be the same God who holds me while I rise. In Jesus' holy name, I pray. Amen.

LLYB Declaration
I Am No Longer Tied To the Pain of My Past

I am tethered to the promise of my healing. I release every lie that told me I had to carry the wound forever. I release shame, bitterness, regret, and the habit of pretending I'm fine when I'm hurting inside. I no longer numb what God is trying to heal. I no longer hide what God is trying to redeem. I give myself permission to feel it, to grieve it, and then to rise from it. I will not confuse survival with wholeness. I was not called to stay broken just because I've learned how to function in fragments. I am healing, fully, deeply, and unapologetically, because I know without a doubt God is not done with me. In fact, He's just getting started. From this day forward, I will speak like restoration is already at work. I believe that every scar will one day be a story of victory. I choose joy even while I wait. I choose peace while I process. I choose hope when the past tries to pull me back. I declare that my healing is not just for me; it's for every woman watching, every child learning, and every room I will walk into with my whole heart intact. I heal like I believe, because I do believe. And I will not stop until every part of me reflects the glory of the One who promises never to leave me.

POWER MOVE 2
LEAD LIKE YOU BELIEVE

"Perhaps you were born for such a time as this."
(Esther 4:14)

Esther had no idea that her path to purpose would begin with intense silence. No trumpet sounded when she lost her parents. No prophecy was given when she became a young Jewish girl placed into the care of her cousin Mordecai. Her name wasn't trending. Her prayers weren't posted. She lived a life most would overlook: quiet, faithful, and hidden in plain sight. Yet, in the invisible realm, *everything* about her life was being perfected.

You see, divine purpose doesn't need applause to be planted. It will grow in secret. Purpose matures in the ordinary. It takes root when no one is watching, so it can rise whole and in power, so that everyone who needs to hear it will.

That was Esther before she became Queen. She didn't grow up in a palace. She wasn't born into privilege. Nevertheless, she was still being prepared, not with swords or scrolls, but with humility, obedience, and the kind of quiet strength that doesn't shrink under pressure. God called her into a moment that would require *all* of it, and more.

The truth is, Esther was taken. Queen Vashti had refused to serve the King and was banished. A royal edict was issued. The King was looking for a new Queen. Esther did not raise her hand to say *pick me*. She was chosen. She would be needed to replace the Queen. Let's be clear. This was not a Hallmark love story. This was a decree—mandatory and merciless.

Young virgins were gathered from across the provinces and brought to the palace. Esther, beautiful, young, and Jewish, was one of them. She didn't have a say. She didn't get to pack a bag. She didn't know if she'd ever see her home again.

I cannot imagine what she was thinking or feeling. I would like to know what her thoughts were as she walked to the palace. Was the air thick with uncertainty? Was everyone staring at her? Did her faith waiver because of the ache of leaving everything familiar and the fear of what was ahead?

She was taken into a system she didn't understand, surrounded by women she didn't know, trained to please a man she'd never met, and all while carrying a secret that could cost her everything: she was Jewish.

Can you feel that? The tension of being seen and unseen at the same time. Of being groomed for greatness while fearing exposure? Wanting to believe there was purpose in the chaos but not knowing how it could unfold. And yet, God was still writing. Even in Babylon. Even in beauty treatments. Even in the brokenness, she was positioned, but not yet activated.

Esther obeyed. She honored the eunuch overseeing her. She followed instructions. She asked for nothing extra. That act of humility helped position her.

The Bible tells us that when the King saw her, something stirred in him. Not just desire, but *delight*. And then she was crowned queen and elevated above every other woman, given the finest robes, the rarest jewels, and the highest seat beside him.

This is the part of the story we all want in our lives. To be seen and wanted by a King. Or so we think. Let's keep dissecting the story of the Queen.

Now, Esther is the Queen, but she was still hidden. Here is the good part and why I chose to include her story. This part of the story is more relatable for "Live Like You Believe."

Her identity is not yet revealed. Her purpose is not yet awakened. Because here is the part most people skip: Being elevated doesn't mean being *activated*. Ask King David. It took about 16 years for him to ascend to the throne, and despite being the King, he still faced troubles and trials.

Sometimes God will place you in the room long before it's time for you to speak. Sometimes the platform comes before the purpose unfolds. This often means there is a waiting period. Sometimes it's days, weeks, or even years. Either way, we must learn how to wait and stay ready. We are encouraged to live faithfully, even when the title feels like a trap.

Esther didn't know it yet, but God had her in position for something far greater than royalty. When the call came, it wouldn't ask for her beauty, but it would demand her bravery.

The Crisis Will Call Us Higher

Queen Esther's crisis came in the form of a man named Haman. Haman was a man drunk on power and burning with hate for the Jewish people. He used his influence to convince the King to issue a decree to destroy *all* of the Jewish people.

When Mordecai (Queen Esther's cousin) heard about the decree, he tore his clothes and sent a message to Queen Esther, begging her to intervene. But Esther was afraid. She knew the law. No one could approach the King without being summoned, not even her, the Queen. To do so meant death, *unless* the King extended his gold scepter. And it had been over a month since she'd seen the King.

Can you imagine that moment? The girl, once taken, was now asked to stand up for the very people she had been told to hide from sight. The crown on her head weighed heavily. It didn't feel like protection; it felt like pressure.

Her response was honest: "I can't go. If I go without being summoned, I could die."

And then Mordecai said the words that echo through history:

"If you remain silent at this time, relief and deliverance will arise from another place... but who knows whether you have come to the kingdom for such a time as this?" (Esther 4:14)

He didn't manipulate her. He simply reminded her. Your crown isn't your covering—*God* is.

This is for all of us. Our silence won't save us; our *obedience* will. Our life is never just about comfort; it is always about *calling*.

Something broke open in Esther's heart. She prayed and then called a fast. The fast would last for three days. No food. No water. No distractions. Just God.

When we don't know what to do, we don't need a plan. We need God's *presence*. We need alignment. We need Heaven's strategy, not man's approval.

When those three days passed, Queen Esther didn't wait for the King to summon her. She stood up, put on her royal robes, and walked toward the throne room, not knowing if she'd walk out again. When the King saw her, favor met her faith, and the scepter rose. Not just because she was beautiful, but because she was *brave*.

This Is the Moment You Have Been Waiting For

The beauty of the story is that Queen Esther didn't just save her people; she saved the entire nation. She stepped fully into who she was always meant to be. She wasn't born for comfort. She was born for impact. She didn't get the crown because she was pretty. She received the crown because she was *positioned* by Heaven.

You, beloved, are no different. You may not feel ready. You may not have all the answers. You may still be carrying the weight of what you didn't choose and the many mistakes you have made. Yet, you *were chosen* anyway.

Not despite your pain, but because you've lived through it. Not because you are perfect, but because you are willing. Not because of your degrees or experience, but because you are fierce. Not to wear a title, but to walk in truth. To help others believe and do the same.

You Were Not Chosen for Ease, You Were Chosen for Impact

There's a Queen Esther inside all of us. The girl who feels unseen. The woman who wonders if she matters. The queen who's afraid to speak. The warrior who is finally ready to rise.

Let this be your moment—the one where you stop waiting for a safer season to be bold. The one where you fast, pray, and *do it anyway.* God has already extended the scepter. Now it's your turn to step into the room and live like you believe.

Questions

1. What part of my identity have I kept hidden to feel accepted, when it may be the very key to my breakthrough?

_____
_____
_____
_____
_____

2. Am I sitting in a position that looks like favor, but avoiding the purpose that comes with it?

3. If I believed I was born for *this exact season*, what decision would I stop postponing today?

Journal Prompt: *Face Your Fears*

There is a day saved on our destiny calendar when hiding is no longer an option, and silence is no longer safe. When God sends a message that disrupts your sleep and your life. When you feel the heat rise in your chest and the fear screams in your ears, and you know in your heart you are called to stand taller. That something is called purpose. That something is legacy. And that something won't wait for perfect conditions; it demands you move anyway.

Esther didn't ask to be queen. She didn't grow up rehearsing palace speeches or political strategy. She was orphaned. Hidden. Quiet. I can imagine she had lots of "what if" questions that were never answered, and perhaps even wondered "why" me. But when the time came, when the fate of her people was at stake, she did the one thing we all must do when fear is present, and our purpose is speaking louder: Queen Esther did it afraid, faced her fears, and led anyway. Because it wasn't just for her survival; it was for saving countless lives. Now it's your turn.

What have you been purposed for that frightens you and causes you to procrastinate? What spaces are you shrinking in, praying that someone else steps up, knowing in your heart that you are the answer?

Please write it down exactly like your soul tells you. Don't spiritualize it. Just own it. Where are you still waiting on a sign when you are the one called to be the sign?

What conversation, business, book, movement, or decision is waiting on your "if I perish, I perish" moment?

Esther didn't need confirmation from three to five of her friends. She chose to answer God's call after praying and fasting. I pray you will do like Queen Esther, and lead like you believe.

_____
_____
_____
_____
_____
_____
_____
_____
_____
_____
_____
_____
_____
_____

Lead Like You Believe

Prayer: For Such a Time as This

Father God,

You are the Author of time. You make no mistakes in where You place us or when You call us. Just like You positioned Esther in a palace not for comfort but for courage, You have placed me in this season for something greater than myself.

Remind me that influence is not about status, it is about surrender. Remind me that favor is not for applause, it is for purpose. Remind me that when I feel afraid or unqualified, You have already gone before me to make a way.

Give me the boldness to speak when silence feels safer. Please give me the discernment to move when the timing is divine. Give me the strength to stand—even if I must do it alone—for what is right, holy, and true.

I know that where You have placed me is sacred. So, I will not shrink. I will not hide. I will not wait for permission to rise. I was made for such a time as this. In the mighty name of Jesus. Amen.

LLYB Declaration
I Am Positioned on Purpose

I am not here by accident. I am not a background character in someone else's story. I am chosen, appointed, and positioned for divine impact. Every door I have walked through, every battle I have faced, and every moment of silence I have endured have prepared me for this moment. I carry wisdom like royalty. I walk in grace like a mantle. I speak truth with love and authority. I do not beg for influence—I steward it. Like Esther, I rise not to be seen, but to make a difference. I do not wait for comfort or certainty. I move when God says move, and I trust that heaven is backing me. My obedience will shift generations. I live like I believe that I was born for this moment.

Power Move 3
Walk Like You Believe

"Your people will be my people, and your God my God."
(Ruth 1:16 NIV)

There is something quietly extraordinary about the way Ruth steps onto the pages of Scripture, not with fanfare or royal lineage, not with the prestige of a bloodline groomed for greatness, but with a grief-soaked resilience and a resolve that seems too pure to be born from anything other than pain.

Her story doesn't begin with triumph or promise. It begins in the ashes of loss: a widow, a foreigner, a woman who had every reason to return to the familiarity of home and heritage but instead stood at the crossroads of comfort and calling and chose the unpaved road of becoming. Ruth was brave.

There is no precedent set for Ruth. No logical reason for her loyalty. No personal gain in following a bitter mother-in-law to a foreign land. But what Ruth teaches us, what she lives with every step she takes as she walks away from Moab, is that transformation never begins in the crowd. It starts in the quiet, gut-wrenching decision to say yes to an unseen God and an unknown future, even when everything around you screams go back to what is safe, known, and culturally acceptable.

Her story is not tender. It's radical. It's the story of a woman who refuses to live a life of inherited limitations.

A woman who looks grief in the face and decides it will not define her. A woman who turns her back on the comfort of cultural conformity and dares to walk into a land where she will have no name, no status, and no guarantee. Just faith, and the quiet whisper of a destiny that is still in seed form.

Letting Go of What Once Gave You Identity

When Ruth uttered the now-iconic words, "Your people will be my people, and your God my God," she wasn't just aligning herself with Naomi, her mother-in-law. She was divorcing every version of herself that no longer aligned with her next season. She was leaving behind the gods of her youth, the customs of her upbringing, the places that knew her maiden name but would never birth her mission. She did so not with fanfare, but with a quiet resolve that speaks louder than any sermon.

Ruth was no longer following comfort; she was choosing covenant. Her decision wasn't about Naomi's promise; it was about God's purpose in her own life.

I have discovered that sometimes, God will wrap your future in the broken remnants of someone else's story, not to test your endurance, but to see if you are willing to follow faith instead of familiarity. God will call you to step forward not in strength, but in surrender, to walk toward your purpose not because it's clear, but because it's *calling*. That is exactly when my spiritual healing began, when I surrendered.

I had to give up my desire to have my life back as it was before my fall, and allow God to restore me to the original version of who He created me to become. It was not easy, but it was so necessary and worth everything.

You cannot become who you're meant to be while still needing to be understood by the people who only know the version of you that made them feel comfortable around you. You cannot walk into your next chapter while clinging to the validation you needed in the last one.

Ruth clearly understood this truth. She knew that staying in Moab would mean preserving what was, but leaving meant partnering with potential and possibilities. She chose forward motion, even when she was afraid.

Becoming Requires the Courage to Be Unknown

When Ruth arrived in Bethlehem, she wasn't welcomed as a daughter of faith. She was viewed as a stranger. An outsider. The woman from Moab. She walked into her new land carrying Naomi's sorrow like a mantle. Her own uncertainty became her shadow. She did not arrive with accolades or applause; she arrived with humility, with hunger, and with the kind of invisible strength that heaven watches in silence.

There was no celebration waiting at the gates. There was no recognition of her sacrifice. There were only whispers. Cold glances. Assumptions. Yet she showed up anyway. She didn't demand space because she knew she would have to earn it. Not through performance, but through perseverance. She wasn't invited to sit at the head table; she was advised to step into the fields.

Becoming Doesn't Happen On Stages. It Happens in Soil.

It is in the unseen places that God does His most visible work. Ruth, who could have crumbled under the weight of obscurity, chose instead to plant her character in the ground. She rose early. She worked late. She gleaned quietly. And while the world debated her worth, Heaven documented her obedience.

Boaz was the Door - Ruth Was Already the Legacy

We have reduced Ruth's story far too often to a romantic tale of boy meets girl. A lot of women say they want a Boaz. A lot of women will not do what Ruth did to attract her Boaz. However, Boaz was not the climax of her story; he was the reward of her courage.

Boaz didn't fall in love with a woman trying to be noticed. He was drawn to a woman who was too busy becoming to worry about being chosen. Ruth did not manipulate her way into purpose. She walked into it with steady hands and unwavering integrity. Boaz, a man of wisdom and honor, simply recognized what had already been established in secret.

When a woman decides to become who God called her to be, she will stop chasing people and start attracting provision. She will stop trying to change to fit in and start commanding the spaces she enters without ever raising her voice. She will stop begging for scraps and begin to harvest her legacy.

Ruth did not become valuable because Boaz saw her. She was already valuable because she had chosen to align her life with a God who could redeem what she lost and multiply what she surrendered. God will do the same for all of His children who live like they believe.

The Birthplace of Becoming

There will always be voices, internal and external, that try to convince you to return to what feels comfortable. To return to what you can explain. To return to the people who remember your struggle but will not recognize your strength.

I know for a fact that you cannot carry the weight of your purpose and the burden of people-pleasing at the same time.

To live like you believe is to accept that you will outgrow places, patterns, people, and even the version of yourself that got you this far. It is to accept that leaving what shaped you is not a betrayal, but a transformation.

Ruth didn't just change her location—she changed her legacy. She entered a land that did not recognize her and became a woman history will never forget. She moved from gleaning to owning. From foreigner to family. From widow to great-grandmother of King David. Not because she chose to fit in, but because she refused to fit in anymore.

Reflection: Permission to Outgrow

A time will come for all of us when fitting in becomes too expensive. When silence costs you your boldness. When shrinking will steal your joy. When the approval of others becomes suffocating. When that time comes, the only thing left to do is heal. Rise out of patterns that kept you predictable. Lead beyond expectations that kept you small. Walk into the wide, open field of becoming messy, vulnerable, sacred, and real. You are not who you were. You do not owe anyone an explanation for evolving.

Questions

1. Are you still trying to be understood in a place God only called you to pass through?

___
___
___
___
___
___
___
___
___

2. What comfort have you been clinging to that is keeping you from the courage to become?

___
___
___
___

3. If you lived like you believed God wanted more for you, what would you release, and where would you go?

Journal Prompt: *Release to Rise*

Write a farewell letter to the version of yourself that stayed small to keep others comfortable. Bless her for surviving. Honor her for enduring. Then tell her goodbye.

Walk Like You Believe

Prayer: Becoming Over Belonging

Gracious and Sovereign God,

Thank You for the example of Ruth—faithful, overlooked, and yet fully aligned with divine purpose. She did not come from a prestigious background, yet you wrote her into the lineage of legacy. She did not fit the mold, but You used her to break the pattern.

Help me to remember that I wasn't created to fit in—I was called to become. When the pressure to conform feels heavy, remind me that Your plans are not limited to public opinion. When I'm tempted to shrink to be accepted, remind me that I'm already approved by You. Give me the courage to walk away from what's familiar when You call me into the unknown. Teach me to value transformation over validation.

I choose to be like Ruth. I choose obedience even when it's quiet. I choose purpose even when it's not popular. I choose the narrow road, the sacred yes, the quiet becoming.

May my loyalty to You outweigh my longing for approval. May I become the woman You have always seen—even when others don't yet recognize her. In the mighty name of Jesus. Amen.

LLYB Declaration
I Was Never Meant to Fit In

I do not conform to culture; I am called to the Kingdom. I do not chase the crowd; I follow the call. I wasn't born to blend in. I was born to become. Like Ruth, I move with purpose, even when it costs me comfort. I walk with conviction, even when no one claps. I say yes to the journey, even when the destination is unclear, because I trust the One leading me.

My value is not diminished by difference. My legacy is not delayed by rejection. I am aligned with heaven's assignment. I walk in the rhythm of God's timing. I live like I believe that not fitting in is the evidence that I am becoming exactly who I was created to be.

Power Move 4
Reach Like You Believe

"Daughter, your faith has made you well. Go in peace and be healed of your affliction." Mark 5:34

    There is a kind of pain that teaches you how to keep moving while bleeding. A sort of ache so persistent and private that it trains you to perform wholeness in public, even while silently falling apart inside. The woman with the issue of blood lived with that kind of pain, not for days, not for weeks, but for twelve long years of being unseen, unheard, and untreated by a world that had no interest in healing what it could not easily diagnose or understand.

    Her illness wasn't only physical; it was emotional, spiritual, and social. She had learned to live in the shadows, avoided by people who once embraced her, marked as unclean by religious law, and pushed to the outskirts of her own story, all while carrying the quiet hope that maybe, someday, something would change. But change, when it takes too long, can begin to sound like a lie whispered by people who don't have to wait for anything.

    By the time we meet her in scripture, she was out of money, resources, explanations, and excuses. But she had not run out of faith, although it was not the polished, rehearsed kind that creates perfect testimonies. Her faith was the desperate, disheveled kind of faith that comes after being disappointed too many times and still believing there's one more chance left to try.

Faith, for her, wasn't an abstract idea. It was not a feeling. It was not even a hope. It was a crawl. It was a stretch. It was a reach. It was the quiet determination kind of reach out and touch something, *anything*, that held power.

It was a belief not in her own strength, which had long since betrayed her, but in the idea that maybe, if she could get close enough to the One whose presence made everything tremble, she could be restored without having to make a scene.

She knew in her heart she had to be strategic, so she didn't draw attention. She only needed to get close for healing, and she was willing to risk everything to get it.

Crawling Becomes an Act of Worship

A few years ago, I was invited to speak at a women's ministry gathering. I had prepared my notes and prayed over my message about the woman with the issue of blood.

Her story is only a few verses long, tucked between miracles and surrounded by crowds. But her faith? Her reach? Her willingness to crawl when standing wasn't an option? That still shakes me.

That evening, I stood in a fellowship hall filled with round tables and folding chairs. No stage. No aisles. Just women—some sipping coffee, some glancing at their Bibles, all carrying something in their hearts.

I opened my Bible and began reading her story aloud. And then, led by the Spirit and stripped of my comfort zone, I got down on the floor. Yes, me, the speaker. Heels off. Mic still on. I got down on my hands and knees, and I began to crawl.

I went from behind the podium to the front and from side to side, around chairs, past polite nods and whispered curiosity. I crawled through the front of the room like she did through the crowd. Slowly. Intentionally. With my heart wide open.

I imagined what she must have felt. Twelve years of bleeding. Of being ignored. Dismissed and labeled unclean. She had no place in the crowd, yet she pushed through anyway. She wasn't after attention. She wasn't trying to be noticed. She was reaching for wholeness. For the hem. For the Healer.

As I reached my hand out in that fellowship hall, toward nothing but air and everything that Jesus is, the room grew still. The women watched. Something holy broke out. Quiet weeping became collective surrender.

I cried too. At first, I couldn't believe I had done that. I crawled on the floor. I made my way back to the podium, not sure what was going to happen next.

Afterwards, they came to me. Some touched my arm. Others hugged me tightly. There wasn't a dry eye in the room, and there wasn't a dry place in my soul.

Here is what I know now. Being humble may cost you your pride, but pride will always cost you your humility. And pride is far too costly.

I know this because I lived it. When I shattered my leg, and with it, my illusion of control and strength, the fall brought me back to the floor, back to the crawl, back to the hem.

There is something sacred about getting low. Something holy in the humility. Something eternal about being so desperate for Jesus that you no longer care who's watching.

That woman in Scripture had already lost everything. Her money. Her status. Her relationships. Her hope. Her pride. She had nothing left to lose. But she had everything to gain. And more than the healing, it was His *response* that makes me weep every time I read it.

Jesus turned and stopped in the middle of the crowd, with people reaching out to him. With needs pressing from every direction, He stopped.

"Who touched me?" He asked, not out of arrogance, but out of intention. He wanted her to know she wasn't just healed, she was seen. She came trembling to Him. He called her "Daughter." Not woman. Not stranger. Not an outcast. Not beggar. *"Daughter."* The identity she didn't even know she still had.

This is the response I long to hear. Not because I need validation, but because I need belonging. I need the assurance that even in my lowest, messiest, most desperate moments, I am still His.

Healing, real healing isn't just about stopping the bleeding or healing broken bones. It's about being named. Known. Claimed. It's about collapsing at His feet and hearing the words that anchor your soul: *"Daughter, your faith has made you well. Go in peace and be freed from your suffering."*

If you're crawling today, if life has knocked the strength out of you, if you've had a fall like mine or a fall no one else has seen, don't despise the floor. You are closer to His hem than you've ever been. He is already turning around to call you *Daughter*.

When Faith Has Nothing to Prove But Everything to Gain

What this woman taught me, and what the woman with the issue of blood embodies, is that faith, at its core, is not about being loud, strong, or polished. It is not about having all the right words or perfect prayers. It's about moving, anyway, even if you have to drag yourself, even if no one else goes with you. Even if people whisper when they see you reach.

Faith is not the absence of doubt. It is the decision to move toward healing even when the pain still pulses in your body and the shame still echoes in your mind.

It is choosing to believe that God's love is not just for the spotless, the put-together, or the ones with unshakable confidence. It is for crawlers. For the broken. For the ones with just enough strength to stretch one last time.

When All You Can Do Is Reach, Reach Anyway

There is a sacred power in reaching when you are exhausted. There is holy ground in the act of pressing forward when the crowd around you reminds you of everything you are not.

What I love most about Jesus in this story is that He stopped. He felt her faith before He even saw her face. He knew healing had left Him before she ever confessed her need aloud. That's the kind of Savior He is, one who responds to the silent reach, who honors the trembling touch, who sees the nameless woman in the crowd and calls her *Daughter*. The same God who stopped for her is still stopping for us.

Reflection: Faith Doesn't Always Look Like Faith

There are moments in life when our strength has nothing left to prove, and everything left to surrender. Moments when our healing doesn't begin with a doctor or a diagnosis, but with the decision to *reach*, even if it's messy, even if it's wordless, even if the miracle is still miles away.

I pray you agree that this chapter isn't just about a woman in scripture. It's about the person reading this right now, who has quietly carried the weight of wounds no one prayed for and victories no one celebrated with us.

You have spent years performing power when you were privately bleeding. You've smiled while slowly unraveling and clapped for others while wondering when your healing would arrive. I salute you! For you are becoming and you are enough!

Questions

1. Where in my life have I grown more comfortable with bleeding silently than risking being seen vulnerably?

_____
_____
_____
_____
_____
_____
_____

2. What pain have I spiritualized or hidden instead of surrendering it to God for healing?

_____
_____
_____
_____
_____
_____

3. Am I more committed to appearing strong than to being made whole? And what will it cost me if I stay that way?

_____
_____
_____
_____
_____
_____
_____

Journal Prompt: *The Stretch Still Counts*

Write without editing. Let this be your crawl, your whisper, your reach. Where have you stopped expecting God to move because the wait hurt more than the wound? What would it mean for you to believe that even your trembling, tired faith is still enough for Him to respond?

Write a love letter from your healed self to the version of you that's still trying to make sense of the pain. Then write one sentence to God that starts with: "Lord, I am reaching again because..."

Reach Like You Believe

Prayer: A Cry from the Crawl

Father God,

I am tired. Not just in my body, but in the deep places I rarely let anyone see. I've bled for years in silence, and though I have learned to live with the pain, I no longer want to.

I no longer want to fake strength while falling apart inside. I no longer want to perform faith when what I need is presence. So today, I reach, not because I have it all together, but because I don't.

I reach through the noise of my thoughts, the ache of my past, the fear of disappointment. I reach through my doubt. I reach through my shame. I reach because I believe, even now, that You are still the God who heals. Touch me in the places no one else can see. Call me daughter again. I believe. Even through the trembling, I believe. In Jesus' name. Amen.

LLYB Declaration
Speak This Over Yourself

Even if I have to crawl, I will move. Even if I have to whisper, I will pray. Even if I have to reach while still bleeding, I will reach. Because I believe that my healing matters to God. I am not invisible. I am not disqualified. I am not too late. I will live like I believe the miracle is already moving toward me.

Power Move 5
Receive Like You Believe

"Two are better than one, because they have a good reward for their labor. For if either of them falls down, one can help the other up. But pity anyone who falls and has no one to help them up." Ecclesiastes 4:9-10

I grew up with the kind of strength that didn't give you permission to fall apart. Not the poetic strength we read about in devotionals, the kind wrapped in beauty and boldness, celebrated and applauded. No, the strength I was taught to model was quiet and unseen. It showed up every day in early morning routines, late-night cleaning, enduring pain silently, and getting the job done, whether anyone noticed or said thank you. It was the kind of strength that swallowed tears in the bathroom mirror and kept moving as if exhaustion was a sign of excellence.

This strength taught me to survive. It got me through long seasons where it seemed I had no one but God to lean on; He is always there. It gave me grit and discipline. But it also gave me something else I didn't ask for, a fear of ever needing help.

The narrative was clear: strong women don't ask. They manage. They lead. They carry. They show up for everyone else and always leave themselves for last.

I believed that if you needed support, it was to admit failure, and that if I were truly spiritual, truly favored, truly capable, I wouldn't have to rely on anyone else to get through.

It wasn't until life got so hard, and I could barely breathe, that I came face-to-face with the lie I had mistaken for truth. Unfortunately, I am a slow learner when it comes to accepting help.

When Letting Others In Is the Strongest Thing You Can Do

There was a time in my life when I thought strength meant never needing help. I was the one who showed up for everyone—the encourager, the prayer warrior, the planner, the rock. I took pride in being the one others could lean on for help. It made me feel purposeful, valued, and seen. But over time, that kind of one-sided strength began to feel more like a prison than a purpose.

It wasn't that I didn't need help; I simply didn't know how to receive it. I had grown so comfortable being the giver that I had unintentionally built an identity around being strong.

Saying "I'm fine" became my default, even when I was far from it. Offers of help felt uncomfortable, not because they weren't genuine, but because I didn't know how to accept them without feeling weak or burdensome.

Then came a season when I was quietly unraveling. I was emotionally drained, spiritually weary, and physically exhausted. I needed rest. I needed help. I needed someone to see me not as the woman who had it all together but as the woman who was holding it together by a thread.

Help came. God sent people who were willing to step in and carry the weight with me. A friend offered to handle an errand. Another asked if she could pray with me. Someone else reached out and asked if they could bring me a meal. Every offer was a lifeline, but I said no.

Not because I didn't appreciate it, but because my pride was still louder than my need. I smiled, thanked them, and told them I was okay when I wasn't okay.

Later that night, as I sat alone with my Bible and my unspoken fatigue, I felt the Spirit nudge my heart with a quiet conviction: "You're not just refusing their help—you're refusing Mine." That stopped me. I quickly replied, "Oh my goodness, Lord, please forgive me."

I had been asking God to send support, to bring relief, to remind me that I was not alone, and when He did, I turned it away—packaged in good intentions, wrapped in independence, hidden behind spiritual language like, "God will provide."

Yes, God will provide. He was sending me help through His people, and I was saying no.

Scripture tells us it is more blessed to give than to receive. It never says we are only called to be givers. We are designed to do both. The kindest people I know are not just generous givers—they are gracious receivers.

We see it throughout the Bible. Elijah, who spoke fire and rain into existence, was fed by a widow.

Paul, the great apostle, wrote to the churches not only with encouragement but with requests for prayer. Even Jesus, who washed His disciples' feet, allowed a woman to anoint His feet.

Receiving is not a weakness. It is wisdom. It is maturity. It is surrender. For far too long, I confused control with strength. Unfortunately, I believed that asking for help made me needy, and being needy meant I wasn't enough. I have since learned that asking for help is not admitting defeat; it is stepping into divine partnership.

Being humbled may cost us our pride, but pride will always cost us the humility necessary to grow. And humility is not humiliation. It is a holy posture.

We miss out on miracles when we refuse to receive help, prayers, and love. One of my friends even said, "Loretta, don't block my blessings, take this blessing."

When we let pride get in the way, we rob others of the opportunity to be obedient to God's prompting by turning down their offer to serve and give. What if our "no thank you" to them is a silent rejection of God's provision?

So now, I say yes. Yes, to help. Yes, to prayer. Yes, to rest. Yes, to the hands extended in love. (I have not completely complied with the act of receiving; however, I am doing better.)

I finally believe that I am worthy not just to pour into others, but also to be poured into. Not because I am broken, but because I am human.

We are called to be both givers and receivers. In learning to receive, I discovered a new kind of strength. One that doesn't have to prove anything. One that doesn't shy away from vulnerability. One who trusts God enough to lean into community.

The same hands I once held out only to give are now open to receive. This shift has changed everything. I now pour from a full cup that is running over with love, peace, and joy.

Even Jesus Asked for Help

As I sat with that truth, something within me changed. I began to reflect on the life of Jesus. The Savior of the world, fully divine and fully human, asked for help. He invited His disciples into His most sacred spaces. He leaned on friends. He asked them to pray with Him in the Garden of Gethsemane. He did not walk through betrayal, agony, and the crucifixion without community. Even as He carried the cross, another man, Simon of Cyrene, was summoned to help bear its weight.

Receive Like You Believe

If Jesus could ask for help in His most painful moments, why couldn't I? Why do many of us, as women of faith, wear exhaustion like a spiritual achievement? Why do we quote "I can do all things through Christ" as if it means we must do *all* things *alone*? That is not what faith looks like. That is not what strength looks like. Faith looks like *receiving*, not just giving. Strength looks like *asking*, not just enduring.

We Were Not Created for Isolation. We Were Created for Connection

God created us for community. He designed us to live in relationship, to bear one another's burdens, to celebrate and cry and lift and grow together. Yet, so many of us isolate ourselves because we're afraid of being judged, misunderstood, or seen as less than capable. But what if we've misunderstood strength all along? What if true strength is found in *trust*, in trusting someone else to show up for us? What if the bravest thing you can do is whisper, "I'm tired," and allow someone to carry you through your weary season? What if living like you believe means believing you are *worth being helped*? Not because you've earned it. Not because you've proven your worth, but simply because you are God's daughter, and your needs are not a bother to Him. They are an opportunity for love to flow back to you.

You Are Not a Burden; You Are a Blessing in the Becoming

You are allowed to ask. You are allowed to rest. You are allowed to stop performing while silently unraveling. I didn't always know that. For so long, I believed I had to hold everything and everyone together—even when I was falling apart. But here is the truth I now live by, the kind of truth that doesn't just comfort, it *frees* us.

Asking for help does not diminish our light. It expands our ability to carry it. It does not define us as weak or unworthy. It does not disqualify us from being called, chosen, or capable. It is not a crack in our strength—it is a doorway that leads us to a deeper grace, the kind that meets us when we have run out of words, out of energy, out of plans, and we finally let go of pride.

I pray that you will live like you believe you're worth supporting—not just when you're performing well or checking every box, but when you're calm, scared, or searching.

Live like you believe your wholeness matters just as much as your work. Live like you believe that God sends help on purpose, to the ones who stop pretending they don't need it, and dare to say, "I can't do this alone." We were never meant to carry every burden or problem all alone.

Reflection: The Truth About Strong Women

Strong women cry. Strong women ask. Strong women receive. We don't lose our strength when we say, "I need you." We reclaim it.

Questions

1. Where in your life are you pretending to be okay when you are clearly carrying too much?

_____
_____
_____
_____
_____
_____

2. What would happen if you lived like you believe that asking for help is holy, not humiliating?

_____
_____
_____

Receive Like You Believe

3. What keeps you from accepting the very gifts you honor in others?

Journal Prompt – *My Freedom to Ask*

Write a letter to the version of yourself who believed she had to do it alone in order to be loved, accepted, or seen as worthy. Speak to her gently but truthfully. Tell her it is safe to let go. Let her know that asking for help is not a sign of weakness but a declaration of faith. Remind her that help is not pity, it is provision sent by a loving God who knows she was never meant to carry everything alone.

Tell her she can stop performing. Tell her she can breathe now. Tell her she is allowed to rest, to ask, and to receive without apology. Then invite her to step into the freedom of being fully supported and fully seen.

Receive Like You Believe

Prayer: Teach Me to Receive

Father God,

You see me. You always have. You know how hard it has been for me to let go of the weight I was never meant to carry alone. I confess—I have made a habit of holding everything together, of being the helper, the giver, the strong one.

Lord, You know my heart. I cannot hide anything from you. Deep down, You know the truth. You know how many times I have quietly needed what I so freely give.

I have turned away help, not because I didn't need it, but because of pride. Forgive me for being prideful. There were times I didn't know how to receive help without feeling small. I have confused independence with identity. I have mistaken asking for help as a weakness. And I've kept pushing forward when all I needed was to pause and let someone hold me up for once. But today, I am choosing differently. Teach me how to receive without guilt. Show me how to accept love without shrinking. Help me believe that when I am supported, I am not less strong—I am more whole. Remind me that vulnerability is not a deficit, but a doorway to deeper grace.

Soften my heart, Lord, and restore the part of me that forgot how to rest. Let me experience the sacredness of being poured into, not because I am broken, but because I am beloved. In the mighty name of Jesus. Amen.

LLYB Declaration
I Will Receive the Grace Assigned to Me

I am not too much. I am not too late. I am not the only one responsible for holding it all together. I do not have to prove my worth by how much I can carry. I reject the lie that receiving is weakness. I embrace the truth that receiving is sacred. I welcome rest. Today, I welcome help. I welcome support sent by God through the people He places in my path. I am worthy of care. I am allowed to pause. I am deserving of peace. I will live like I believe that grace flows to the one who gives *and* to the one who dares to receive.

Power Move 6
Trust Like You Believe

"Be still and know that I am God." Psalm 46:10

There is a quiet kind of grief that never announces its arrival. It does not wail, storm, or shatter windows. It simply settles into the in-between spaces of your everyday, and little by little, convinces you to disappear while still going through the motions of being alive.

It creeps in while you're busy replying to emails, folding laundry, showing up for appointments, and scrolling through a hundred other people's highlight reels. Before you know it, you've become a beautifully composed version of yourself who is rarely, if ever, fully present in her own life.

You walk into rooms but leave your mind behind. You listen to people you love with half of your attention and all of your anxiety. You smile, but it feels forced, because it belongs to a different version of you, the one who used to love without holding back. You used to dream without asking for permission, used to cry without shame, and breathe without guilt.

There is a persistent ache that comes with being physically visible yet emotionally distant. What makes it more serious than any heartbreak is how easily it hides behind a facade of productivity.

No one questions the woman who is always busy, who keeps her calendar full, and who gets things done.

She is praised for her efficiency. She is applauded for her strength. But the truth, the part no one sees, is that she cannot remember the last time she sat in a room and actually *felt* happy. It is difficult to remember the last time she touched her own skin without flinching at what she's been carrying. When was the last time she heard her own thoughts and didn't try to drown them out with noise?

She has confused motion with meaning. She has confused function with fulfillment. She has forgotten that the most sacred place God meets us is not in our next breakthrough, not in the future we keep chasing, but in the presence we keep abandoning.

Sometimes Stillness Feels Like Punishment, but Silence is Actually Protection

There was a time, while dealing with my broken leg, when God, in His mercy, allowed everything to pause, not gently, but forcefully. I was no longer able to move at the pace I had once prided myself on. I could not serve, host, create, fix, produce, or control.

At first, I resisted it as if it were a punishment for something I hadn't done. I mistook stillness for suffering because I had built a life that ran on the validation of being needed.

The irony is that when the movement stopped and the noise faded, I could finally hear what I had ignored for years: my own pain. My own joy. My own voice. God's voice. No thundering or theatrical. Just steady, loving, patient, and kind.

In the slowness, I could feel how disconnected I had become from myself, how numb I was to the beauty that surrounded me daily, how addicted I had been to doing so that I never had to just *be*.

Simply *being* is difficult. Being requires honesty. And honesty reveals how many pieces of myself I had scattered across obligations and overcommitments. The many years I had spent being who I thought I needed to be in order to prove I was worthy of love, respect, and divine favor. It wasn't just physical rest I needed; it was *sacred remembrance.* I needed to return to the woman I had buried beneath busyness.

The Present Is Where Your Life Actually Lives

We say things like "I'll slow down once this is done," or "I'll enjoy life after the next goal is met," but what we fail to realize is that life is not holding its breath, waiting for us to catch up. It is happening now. Life is expanding in the quiet moments we rush past, in the conversations we half-hear, in the way the sunlight dances on the wall when we take a minute to pause and look up.

Joy does not live on the other side of our checklists. Healing does not wait for a permission slip. Peace is not a future event that we can schedule on our calendars. Peace is Him, and His presence is here. NOW. But if we continue to live in yesterday's guilt or tomorrow's anxiety, we will always miss the miracle of what God is doing today, right now, in this moment.

Being present is not just a therapeutic exercise; it is a spiritual discipline that requires the courage to face the parts of ourselves we're afraid to acknowledge. When we slow down and breathe deeply into our own being, we stop performing for love and begin receiving love. We stop surviving our days and begin living them. We stop measuring our worth by how much we accomplish and remember that our existence, right here and right now, is already proof that we are still chosen, still carried, still enough.

Reflection: You Are Already Worth Showing Up For

Maybe your story, like mine, has seasons of withdrawal, times where you went on autopilot to protect yourself, times where presence felt unsafe, times where you numbed your feelings just to make it through. If so, I want you to know this: you are not behind. You are not lost. You are still reachable. You can come home to yourself without shame.

Presence is not about perfection. It is about permission. Permission to slow down, to feel, to receive. Permission to reconnect with that version of you that God still delights in, even when you have forgotten how to find your way back to a healthier and happier version of yourself. Your soul has been waiting patiently for your return.

Questions

1. In what areas of my life am I physically present but emotionally or spiritually disconnected? What am I protecting by staying that way?

_____
_____
_____
_____
_____
_____
_____

2. What are the patterns, habits, or distractions I use to keep myself from feeling what I most need to acknowledge?

_____
_____
_____
_____
_____
_____
_____

3. What would it look like to give myself permission to enjoy where I am without waiting for conditions to improve?

Journal Prompt: *A Letter to My NOW*

Write a letter to the present version of yourself, the one who has done her best to hold it all together, who has given more than she's received, who has been strong for everyone else but hasn't sat with her own heart in far too long.

Tell her she's safe now. Tell her she's worthy of peace that doesn't have to be earned. Tell her she can exhale. Remind her that she is still here, and that being here is enough.

Trust Like You Believe

Prayer: I Want to Be Here, God

Father God,

I confess I've been showing up everywhere except the present. I've been checking boxes, filling roles, and doing the work of being human, but I've missed You in the very place You have always been, which is right here in the now. Teach me to notice. Teach me to slow down. Teach me to sit with what I have been avoiding.

Help me hear my own breath again. Help me to delight in moments I used to rush. Help me to forgive myself for missing so much, and love myself enough to stop missing what's still here. Today, I return to myself. To this moment. To You. It is in the sweet name of Jesus Christ, my Lord and Savior. Amen.

LLYB Declaration
I Choose Presence Over Performance

I am no longer rushing through my life as if joy is waiting for me somewhere else. I will no longer numb the present to protect myself from the pain of what has passed or the fear of what's coming. I choose to be here, not perfectly, but fully. I choose stillness, not as surrender to defeat, but as a return to God's rhythm for my life. This moment is a gift from God. This breath is sacred. I will live like I believe that *now* is enough.

POWER MOVE 7
FORGIVE LIKE YOU BELIEVE

"You intended to harm me, but God intended it for good to accomplish what is now being done, the saving of many lives." Genesis 50:20 (NIV)

Forgiveness is one of those truths that sounds beautiful in theory but sometimes feels impossible when you're the one who's been betrayed.

We like to talk about letting "it" go, but what do you do when the thing you're trying to release still echoes in your heart at night? When the hurt didn't just bruise your ego, but fractured your trust, confidence, and identity? When the person who wounded you was the same one who was supposed to love you?

Joseph's reality was similar to what some of us have experienced. His story is often pictured as a tale of destiny, of a boy with a dream who became a man with power. But before the throne, before the favor, before the reunion, there was pain and betrayal. There was the pit. There was a time when the people he trusted most didn't just doubt him, they discarded him.

Those people were his brothers. Blood. Family. The ones who knew his face, knew his voice, shared his childhood. And when jealousy crept in, when his dream became too much for them to handle, they conspired, not just to silence him, but to erase him. They didn't just mock him. They threw him into a pit, stripped him of his coat, and sold him like he was nothing more than a transaction. Then they went home, carrying the lie and the guilt, pretending that they didn't know what happened to him. How do you forgive *that*?

Forgiveness Hurts Most When It's Personal

It is one thing to be hurt by strangers, but it's another to be broken by the hands you once held.

Betrayal, when it comes from someone you love, doesn't just cut; it reshapes you. It makes you question your instincts. It makes you question your voice. It makes you wonder if you missed the signs or if you somehow deserved the hurt. It rewrites your memory, casting shadows over once-cherished moments.

Joseph didn't ask for any of the pain and heartache. He didn't provoke it. He simply believed too boldly, spoke too freely, and trusted too deeply. And for that, he was punished.

His brothers didn't just hurt him; they altered the course of his life. Yet years later, when Joseph had every right and every resource to retaliate, he didn't seek vengeance.

Joseph didn't expose them in front of Pharaoh's court. He didn't imprison them as they had once done to him. He wept. He embraced them. He *forgave them*. And he cared for them.

Forgiveness is Not a Weakness, It's Bold Faith

Forgiveness isn't about acting as if it didn't happen. It isn't about moving on or pretending the pain dissolved. Forgiveness is the brave, spiritual decision to no longer let someone else's actions control your story.

Forgiveness is not the approval of what they did—it is the release of what they still hold.

When Joseph said, "You intended to harm me, but God intended it for good," he wasn't excusing their betrayal. He was choosing his *peace* over their *power*.

Here's what most people miss: forgiveness is not about making the other person feel better. It's about setting yourself free. It's about closing the door to bitterness so that healing can walk in. It's about refusing to carry the weight of what they did into the promise of what God is still doing.

Joseph forgave not because his brothers apologized perfectly. He forgave because his destiny was too important to be delayed by bitterness.

God Will Still Use What They Meant to Break You

One of the most profound truths I've learned through pain is that forgiveness does not start when the other person apologizes. It starts with a decision to stop rehearsing what hurt you and start reclaiming what God promised you.

I have learned to be okay and forgive even if the person does not apologize. I have had to forgive without ever hearing the words, "I'm sorry." I have had to forgive when I still felt betrayed. I've had to forgive when my heart was still broken.

I had to do it. Not because they earned it, but because I was ready to break free from what they did. Forgiveness was the only thing my soul needed to release the person from my mind and my heart. It was the key I didn't know I had, unlocking the room where I had imprisoned my peace.

It was me choosing to *live like I believe* that my story wasn't over, and that nothing they did could override what God had destined for me.

Joseph's story can remind us that even the worst betrayal can be woven into a greater purpose. That pit? It became the place where his character was tested and his trust in God was forged. That prison became the training ground for leadership. His brothers? They became the very people he would later protect and provide for in the midst of famine. Only God could write a redemption story that poetic.

You Deserve Peace, Even If They Never Say Sorry

Forgiveness is hard because it feels like we're letting someone off the hook. But what if you're the one still hanging on it? What if the apology you've been waiting for is not coming, but your healing doesn't have to wait? What if you gave yourself permission to stop needing closure and started embracing *freedom*?

Let me be honest with you, there are people in our lives who will never admit they were wrong. They may never change. They may never confess. Waiting for their apology is like waiting for rain in a drought. You can't keep putting your peace on pause, waiting for someone else to change.

Forgiveness is more than a transaction. It is actually transformation. You let go so you can live. You forgive so you can move forward, unburdened and unbothered.

Live Like You Believe Forgiveness is Your Liberty, Not Their Reward

When you choose to forgive, you are choosing to *live like you believe* that your purpose matters more. You are choosing to honor your future instead of staying chained to a painful past.

Joseph didn't have to open his arms to his brothers. He didn't have to invite them into safety and provision. But when he did, redemption and restoration took place.

Your story is far from being over. What happened to you will not be the final chapter. The enemy may have tried to use betrayal to derail your destiny, but God is the author and finisher of our story, and He will not waste a single sentence. You can forgive. Not because it's easy, but because you are ready to live life more abundantly.

Reflection: The Release That Heals

You do not have to pretend it didn't hurt. You do not have to forget what they did. You only need to remember that *you are not what happened to you*. You are healing. You are the hope. You are the story of forgiveness wrapped in flesh. Forgiveness is not erasing the past. It's choosing to no longer let it define your future. Your heart has carried the weight long enough. Let today be the day you set it down.

Questions

1. What part of your identity have you unconsciously tied to a painful memory, and who would you become if you released that pain today?

_____
_____
_____
_____
_____
_____

2. Have you confused forgiveness with reconciliation, and is that belief keeping you from claiming the peace you were always meant to walk in?

_____
_____
_____
_____
_____
_____
_____

3. If you truly believed that nothing done to you could cancel what God has destined for you, how would that shift the way you view those who hurt you?

Journal Prompt: *I Forgive to Be Free*

Who are you still tethered to through pain, resentment, or unmet expectations? What belief is keeping you from releasing the hurt? (e.g., "If I forgive them, it means they win.") In what ways has unforgiveness been silently affecting your joy, peace, or ability to trust again? Write a letter to the person you are ready to forgive, not to send, but to release. Let the words fall honestly, tearfully, and completely.

Forgive Like You Believe

Prayer: The Courage to Forgive

Father God,

You know how heavy the burden of unforgiveness can be for me. You've seen the silent tears and the guarded smiles. You've heard the prayers I prayed through gritted teeth—wanting to release the pain but still holding onto the memory of what was done.

Lord, I want to forgive, but sometimes it feels like forgiving means forgetting, excusing, or pretending it didn't hurt. And it did hurt. Deeply.

But today, I choose freedom over resentment. I choose healing. I choose obedience over emotional comfort because You didn't just call me to forgive for their sake, you called me to forgive so I could be forgiven.

Teach me how to release the offense without reliving the trauma. Help me trust that vengeance belongs to You, and justice does not require my constant rehearsal of the pain.

Soften the parts of my heart that have hardened to survive. And remind me that forgiveness is not me losing, but about me letting go so I can finally heal.

Let Your love be louder than the memory. Let Your peace run deeper than the wound. Let Your Spirit walk with me as I do the holy, hard, and healing work of forgiveness. In the mighty name of Jesus. Amen.

LLYB Declaration
Forgiveness Is My Freedom

I walk in the fullness of freedom because I choose to forgive. I carry peace, not because the past didn't hurt, but because I no longer allow it to define me. My heart is open, my spirit is strong, and my future is unchained from what tried to keep me bound. Forgiveness is not a favor I extend; it is a boundary that I establish for my own healing. It clears space for joy, clarity, and growth. I release what no longer serves the woman I am becoming. I make room for wholeness, for restoration, and for God's justice to speak louder than revenge ever could. My identity is rooted in grace. My posture is one of power. And my peace is non-negotiable. I live like I believe that nothing from my past has permission to poison my purpose.

Power Move 8
Give Like You Believe

The Art of Seed, Surrender, and Overflow
"Give, and it will be given to you. A good measure, pressed down, shaken together, and running over, will be poured into your lap. For with the measure you use, it will be measured to you." Luke 6:38

Giving has often been reduced to an act of charity, something we do when we feel generous, when we have more than we need, or when we're in the mood to be kind.

For those who walk by faith, giving was never meant to be a task, a guilt offering, or a strategic play for public affirmation. It was intended to be a declaration, an intimate, sacred statement that says, *I trust God more than I trust the safety of my own supply.*

Some people have become so conditioned to believe that giving is about subtraction that every time something leaves their hands, they feel as though they are left with less.

However, in the Kingdom of God, giving is never about loss; it is about unlocking what is already assigned to us in the supernatural.

Giving is not a deduction from our lives; it is an expansion of our faith, our perspective, and our participation in the miraculous.

When we give, not just of our finances, but of our love, our time, our energy, our wisdom, our creativity, and our compassion, we are practicing the art of surrender.

We are placing our seeds into the soil of eternity, trusting that what we release will not vanish but will return multiplied, refined, and more powerful than we could have ever imagined. God always uses multiplication.

Let me tell the truth. Most of us don't struggle to give because we don't want to be generous. We struggle to give because we fear we won't have enough left. Enough to rest. Enough to cover the bills. Enough to feel safe. Enough to keep going.

Somewhere along the way, we were taught that holding tightly would protect us, that keeping it all to ourselves was how we stayed in control. But genuine giving is not rooted in control. It is rooted in *belief*. Giving asks us to trade in the illusion of self-sufficiency for the reality of divine partnership.

The Invisible Principle of the Seed

Everything God created, every law of nature, every spiritual principle, every mystery of multiplication, starts with a seed. We may have heard this all our lives, but how many of us live like we believe it? That the miracle we are praying for might already be in our hands, just in seed form?

Joy is a seed. Forgiveness is a seed. Prayer is a seed. Encouragement is a seed. Finances are seeds. And the thing about seeds is this: they only reveal their purpose *after* they are released.

A seed held onto too tightly will never fulfill its destiny. It will never multiply. It will never bear fruit. It will never become a tree that provides shade, shelter, or nourishment.

However, once it is planted, once it is surrendered into the soil of trust, it begins to break, to open, to die to its original form so it can rise into something it never could have become on its own.

This is what giving does. It breaks us open. It pulls us out of fear. It challenges our dependency on control. And in that process, it makes us accessible to miracles.

God never asks for the seed without already knowing what the harvest will look like. You don't have to understand how it will return. You only need to be faithful enough to sow.

The Giver Who Moved Heaven

There's a short moment in Scripture that most would pass over without much thought, but I believe it holds one of the most powerful lessons on giving in the entire Bible.

In Mark 12, Jesus sits near the temple treasury, observing the crowd as they offer their money.

The rich pour in large sums with ease, giving from their abundance, their overflow, their profits. Then, without fanfare, without applause, and without title, a poor widow steps forward and drops in two copper coins, everything she had to live on.

To the casual onlooker, her offering meant nothing. It wouldn't move the needle. It wasn't impressive. But Jesus didn't just notice her, He stopped everything to highlight her. He didn't praise the wealthy with their flashy giving. He praised her because she gave, not out of convenience, but out of faith.

Jesus saw what no one else did. He saw the heart behind the gift. He spoke truth that confirms through generations: she gave *more* than all the rest. Not because the amount was greater, but because the sacrifice was deeper. She believed God would sustain her after her offering, and that belief moved Heaven.

The Surrender That Builds Legacy

There have been many years in my life when I gave while broken. I gave time to people who forgot me the moment they no longer needed me. I gave resources to causes I believed in, even when my own expenses didn't add up.

There were times when I gave encouragement while silently fighting discouragement myself. I gave love to people who didn't always reciprocate it. And still, I gave. Not to be seen. Not to be repaid. But because giving has become my act of worship.

I learned that giving when it makes sense is *kindness*. But giving when it defies logic? That's *faith*. That's saying to God, "I trust You more than my math." That's living like you believe that Heaven is not just aware of your offering but is keeping a record of it every time. I can promise you, God does not forget what we give in faith.

When you give, you are not just making a donation. You are sowing a declaration. *My God will supply all my needs according to His riches, not mine. (Philippians 4:19)* My harvest will come from my obedience, not my comfort. Giving is more than an action; it is an alignment with God's way of doing things.

Overflow Is Not a Coincidence, It's a Covenant

We have been conditioned to believe that overflow is rare, random, or reserved for the lucky or the privileged. But in the Kingdom, overflow is not based on status. It is based on *faith*. God does not bless us in spite of our giving. He blesses us *because* of it.

Luke 6:38 is not poetry; it's a promise. When you give, it will be given to you. Not just a little. Not just getting back what you gave. But a good measure, pressed down, shaken together, and running over, poured into your lap by the hands of a God who keeps His word.

Give Like You Believe

This kind of overflow doesn't always look like extra money. Sometimes it's an unexpected blessing. Sometimes it's in the form of restored relationships. Sometimes it's opportunities you couldn't have created, wisdom you couldn't have earned, peace you couldn't have purchased. Whatever it looks like, the promise remains: your seed *will* return.

Reflection: Generosity Isn't Loss, It's Legacy

Every time you give, you are choosing to write a future for someone else. Every time you open your hand, you are expanding your heart. Every time you release what you were tempted to grip, you are making room for something greater. You don't have to be rich to be generous. You just have to believe that generosity is not a loss, but an investment in something that will outlive you.

Questions

1. What is something God may be asking you to release, but you've been holding onto it out of fear that there won't be enough for you?

_____
_____
_____
_____
_____
_____
_____

2. Have you ever given from a place of trust rather than abundance, and what did that experience reveal about your faith?

_____
_____
_____
_____

GIVE LIKE YOU BELIEVE

3. If you truly believed every seed you sowed in obedience would return to you in divine favor, how would that change the way you give today?

Journal Prompt: *My Seeds Will Not Be Wasted*

Reflect on the areas where you have hesitated to give, whether it's your time, your gifts, your energy, or your finances. What fears have kept your hands closed?

Write down one area in your life where you want to see a harvest. Identify the seed you can sow into that area. Think of someone or something you can bless this week without recognition or reward. Give quietly, generously, and with intention.

Give Like You Believe

Prayer: Give Like You Believe

Gracious Father,

Thank You for trusting me with the ability to give. Thank You for the gifts, the resources, the compassion, and the time that I have been called to steward well. I recognize that giving is not an obligation, but an opportunity to reflect on Your heart. You are the ultimate Giver, and I want to give like I believe You are still multiplying what leaves my hands.

Teach me how to give without fear of lack. Make me a cheerful giver, not just in finances, but in love, encouragement, grace, and time.

Remind me that what I release into the lives of others never returns void when done in obedience and love.

Open my eyes to see where I am needed. Open my hands so that nothing is clenched in fear. And open my heart to trust You with the outcome.

Let my giving be joyful. Let it be led by the Holy Spirit. Let it be generous, not performative. And let it glorify You in every way. In the mighty name of Jesus. Amen.

LLYB Declaration
I Give with Heaven's Confidence

I give because I trust that God multiplies what I surrender. I give because I believe there is always more because God is my source. I give because generosity does not create loss; it makes a legacy. My gifts are not small when placed in the hands of a big God. Every seed that I sow is an act of faith. Every word of encouragement, every moment of service, every financial offering is a divine transaction between heaven and earth. I give boldly. I give joyfully. I give with eternity in mind. I live like I believe that the more I pour out in love, the more heaven pours into me.

POWER MOVE 9

RISE LIKE YOU BELIEVE

"Though I fall, I will rise again. Though I sit in darkness, the Lord will be my light." Micah 7:8 (NLT)

There is a kind of quiet attrition that happens to a woman who has spent years navigating the expectations of others while trying to preserve a piece of herself.

It doesn't come suddenly, like an earthquake that levels everything in one strike, but slowly, subtly, like waves lapping at the edges of her soul, gently convincing her that her power is too loud, her presence too wide, her truth too complicated, her joy too much.

Over time, without even realizing it, she learns to round off the edges of her personality, to soften the colors of her confidence, and to carefully edit the full expression of her becoming.

She tells herself she is making peace and being wise. But what she is really doing is abandoning her original version to become a lesser version of herself. She is dimming her light so that others can feel more comfortable around her, not all at once, but in tiny proportions each time.

She learns how to tiptoe in rooms where she was born to stride. She chooses silence over confrontation, not because she lacks words, but because somewhere along the way, she internalized the belief that her truth would cost too much. She has been taught that fitting in is a form of POWER. That shrinking keeps things smooth. That if she just smiles more, agrees more, gives more, and needs less, she will be loved. She will be kept. She will be safe. So, she adapts. She diminishes. The tragedy is not just that she disappears to others, but that she disappears to herself.

There is no peace in a life built on performance. There is no safety in a version of yourself that only exists to preserve someone else's comfort. There is only spiritual starvation. An internal pain that cannot be named, only felt, like a grief that has no hope.

The truth is this: when you shrink to be loved, the love you receive will never satisfy you, because it is not loving the real you. It is loving the impostor. The performance. The contortion. And deep down, you know it is not you they love, and it hurts.

Unraveling the Lie That You Must Shrink to Belong

There comes a divine moment in every woman's life when she begins to sense the weight of her own silencing. It may arrive through the slow exhaustion of never being fully known, or in the sadness that creeps in when you realize people love your presence but have never heard your voice.

It may come as a jolt, a question you didn't ask for but can no longer ignore: *What would it feel like to be fully seen, and still fully loved?*

And so, begins the unraveling. Not a reckless rebellion, but a righteous return. A return to the truth of who you were before the world told you who to be. Before culture assigned you a role. Before religion misinterpreted humility as invisibility. Before survival convinced you that your softness made you weak, and your strength made you a threat.

This return is messy. It will not fit neatly into the life you built while hiding from yourself. It will disrupt the dynamics that depended on your silence. It will unsettle the people who benefited from your pretending.

Then it will also make room for peace, real peace, not the kind you negotiated for by abandoning yourself, but the kind that floods in when your body, mind, and spirit finally come into alignment with who God says you are. It is the peace that says, *"This is who I am. This is how I love. This is how I lead. And I will no longer apologize for living my life like I believe, I am more than enough."*

Healing Begins the Moment You Stop Performing

It is difficult to heal in the same space where you were required to hide. Healing demands space. It demands truth. It demands presence. It cannot happen in the shadows of your own life. It cannot begin while you are still more committed to being accepted than being whole.

To live and love like you believe means you no longer define your worth by how quiet you are or how little you require. You honor your presence, speak with purpose, and embrace the truth that you were created to lead, to impact, and to thrive without apology.

It means you stop apologizing for your brilliance. It means you stop making yourself small to fit into someone else's limited definition of appropriate, likable, or safe. It means you trust that the God who created you in fullness never once asked you to dim what He designed to shine. It means you will be misunderstood. Yes, you will be criticized. Yes, they'll say you've changed, and they'll be right because you have. Yet, this time, it's not for their comfort. It's for your growth. It's for your healing. It's for your good. And you're not going back.

Healing will make you unrecognizable to the old version of you that was built on fear. Be mindful that this version of you will draw new people to you and cause some family and friends to disassociate with you. Please be okay with this process. I refer to it as "growing pains."

My Personal Story: Shrinking While Evolving

People would never believe that there was a season in my life when I started shrinking, and it became my alter ego.

Shrinking became my default, my quiet way of fitting in, of not drawing attention, of making sure everyone else stayed comfortable. I did it so often, for so long, it started showing up as anxiety and mild panic attacks, both of which, I now know, are just symptoms of fear wearing a different mask.

I had mastered the art of being composed on the outside—poised, prepared, pleasant. But inside, there was often a storm I dared not name. I never experienced a full-blown panic attack because I learned to leave before it reached that point.

If I walked into a room and couldn't see a window or an exit, something inside me would start to tighten. My soul would whisper what my heart couldn't say: *You need to get out of here.* And so, I did. If there were no windows or exit doors near me, I quietly slipped out of meetings. I declined invitations. I avoided events that looked powerful on paper but felt unsafe to my nervous system.

People saw my smile, but they didn't see the strategy behind it. I still recognize the signs: the shallow breath, the inner trembling, the compulsive need to know how to leave.

However, through prayer, intentional breathing, and reframing my thoughts, I have learned to stay rooted. I can now talk myself into staying instead of retreating. But on one particular day, it took more than my own voice to stay grounded.

Rise Like You Believe

A small group of us were walking toward the elevators inside the Tennessee State Capitol, on our way to witness one of my friends being sworn in on the House floor.

This was a once-in-a-lifetime kind of moment. The kind you dress up for, pray over, and remember for years. I had been invited to witness it front and center, seated among state representatives on the floor of the House Chamber. But before we even reached the elevators, the tunnel began to close in on me. I couldn't see any windows. I couldn't see the exit doors.

My breathing grew shallow, my vision tunneled, and that all-too-familiar thought returned: *I need to leave.* I leaned toward my best friend and whispered, "I don't think I can do this. I'll wait for you in the car."

I was already playing out my quiet exit. I would smile, wave, and disappear, just like I had done so many times before. *Better to leave than to unravel,* I thought. *Better to miss a moment than to lose control.*

However, before I could act on that instinct, a young woman I hadn't noticed stepped beside me. She gently took my hand and spoke so softly I almost missed it.

"Don't leave," she said. "You don't want to miss this."

There was no judgment in her voice. No pressure. Just a calm presence. She started talking about the architecture of the Capitol, how beautiful the portraits were, how historic the building felt, and how the upper levels had windows and doors. As she spoke, she walked with me, gently guiding me forward, one step at a time, through the tunnel.

She didn't try to fix me. She simply *stayed* with me. That changed everything.

I began to pray with every step I took. *Lord, help me keep walking. Help me stay.* I whispered the name of Jesus under my breath. With every forward movement, panic loosened its grip.

We reached the elevator. Then the stairs. Then the House floor. Until I was standing at the center of a sacred, historical moment, not as a spectator from the sidelines, but as someone fully present and fully placed by God.

If I had left, I would have missed it all. I would have missed witnessing my friend's powerful swearing-in ceremony and taking photos with her.

I would have missed the opportunity to connect with lawmakers, shake hands with leaders, and receive words of encouragement from people who saw something in me. I would have missed the affirming joy that came from knowing I chose presence over panic.

And that young woman, I will never forget her. She didn't need a title or a microphone to shift the atmosphere. She used kindness and proximity to reroute my entire day.

God used her hand to steady mine, and her words to break the cycle I had been trapped in until then. That day, I learned something I now carry everywhere I go: *Sometimes fear shows up first, but it doesn't get the final say. I am in control.*

God reminded me that I was not created to silently retreat from rooms He had prepared for me. I was created to *remain*, even when I feel unsteady, even when there is no door in sight, even when my past tries to convince me that my safety is in hiding.

I no longer measure peace by proximity to the exit. I measure peace by proximity to God's presence that is always with me, whether I am in a boardroom, a broadcast studio, or the center of the House floor.

Becoming the Woman You Are Meant to Be

The process of becoming the fullest version of yourself is not a glow-up. It is a soul-deep reconstruction. It will ask you to confront the stories you've told to stay safe. It will require you to grieve the friendships that only survived when you didn't speak your truth.

It will challenge your loyalty to environments that depend on your conformity. It will call you to release the guilt you've carried for simply being *more* than what others could understand. But here is the divine promise woven into your release: *you will rise.*

You will rise with a new tenderness that is not fragile, but fierce. You will rise with a love that is not performative but rooted. You will rise with a voice that trembles at first, but ultimately roars.

You will rise with a self-knowing that allows you to love others deeply without losing yourself in the process. You will rise into the version of yourself that no longer apologizes for taking up space, but sees it as a stewardship.

Living and Loving Without Permission Slips

To live and love like you believe is to stop waiting for permission to be powerful. It is to take up space, not with arrogance, but with the kind of holy assurance that knows your presence is not an accident.

It is to walk into rooms not wondering if you belong, but declaring internally, *I enter this space to both give and gather light, knowing we're all part of something greater.*

It is to extend love generously, but not at the cost of your own voice. It is to remain soft without becoming silent. It is to choose joy, not as a personality trait, but as a protest against the narratives that say you could only be taken seriously if you suffered silently.

You are not "too much." You are the exact expression of God's creativity, wrapped in strength, softness, wisdom, and holy passion. You are the healing you have been waiting to find in others. You are the safe space you have longed for. You are the woman who finally believed she didn't need to be smaller to be sacred.

Reflection: I Take Up Space Unapologetically

You do not have to be brash to be bold. You do not have to be loud to be luminous.

Simply be unflinchingly, unapologetically true to the woman God designed when He looked at the world and said, *"What I'm about to create will carry light."*

You are not selfish for protecting your peace. You are not egotistical for being proud of your growth. You are not rebellious for choosing authenticity over approval.

You are whole. You are radiant. You are called. You are enough, not because you finally fit in, but because you finally stood tall.

Questions

1. Where have you been performing a smaller version of yourself in exchange for acceptance? What has it cost you over time?

_____
_____
_____
_____
_____
_____
_____

2. What fears surface when you imagine being fully seen and fully honest? Are those fears rooted in truth or trauma?

_____
_____
_____
_____
_____
_____
_____

3. If you could rewrite your story from this moment forward, where the central character is no longer shrinking but shining, what would her next chapter say?

___

Journal Prompt: *This Is Me*

Write down one environment, relationship, or internal belief that has made you feel like you are too much. How have you adjusted yourself to stay accepted in that space? Describe the woman who emerges when you no longer make yourself smaller. What does she do? How does she speak? What does she no longer tolerate? Create a vision for the life you would live if you no longer apologized for who you are. Who would benefit from the real you showing up consistently?

___

Rise Like You Believe

Rise Like You Believe

_____

_____

_____

Prayer: I Will No Longer Disappear

Father God,

You have never called me to disappear. You formed me with intention. You gave me presence, power, and purpose. But somewhere along the way, I began to believe that staying small was safer. I started shrinking, not out of humility, but out of fear.

Lord God, I tried to make myself less visible so others would feel more comfortable. I thought peace meant staying quiet. But all it did was make me anxious in rooms where I was meant to stand in truth.

Father, I surrender the need to manage other people's comfort at the expense of my own calling. I release the habit of retreating when You have called me to remain.

I repent for the times I trusted fear more than I trusted Your presence.

Thank You for never leaving me even in the tunnels of anxiety and the silence of panic. Thank You for whispering peace when my heart wanted to flee. Thank You for using strangers, sacred moments, and quiet courage to remind me that I belong.

Please give me the strength to stay. Not just physically, but emotionally, mentally, and spiritually. Let me be fully present in the rooms You open.

Let me be grounded in peace even when I don't see an exit. Let me walk in with calm confidence, because I know I am not alone, for You are always with me. In the mighty name of Jesus. Amen.

LLYB DECLARATION
I STAND IN PEACE AND LEAD WITH PRESENCE

I carry peace into every room because I no longer question if I belong. I lead with calm confidence, knowing that I am not here by accident. I am positioned on purpose. I no longer make myself small to protect others from my presence. I honor the voice God gave me, the wisdom He shaped in me, and the power He placed within me. I trust His timing. I remain steady, even when the path feels unfamiliar. I remain open, even when my old fears whisper otherwise. I remain present because this moment is sacred. So am I. I live like I believe that peace is not found in the exit, but in the presence of the One who walks in with me.

POWER MOVE 10
PRAY LIKE YOU BELIEVE

"Don't just speak to God like He's listening—pray like you know He's already moving." Loretta McNary

Let's be honest, too many of us pray as if God is on a tight budget. Whispering timid requests into the sky, hoping not to be too much of a bother. We pray like we are renters in the Kingdom instead of daughters with the keys. We pray like we are unsure if we deserve an answer. We pray like God is eavesdropping, not listening. But listen to me—no more. No more bargaining prayers. No more faithless repetition. No more apologies for asking. If the same God who spoke galaxies into orbit is the one who says, "Ask and it shall be given," then why are we praying like we're tiptoeing through broken glass?

This move right here? This is about reclaiming your voice. Your authority. Your identity as a woman whose prayers don't just rise—they roar. Because when you Pray Like You Believe, heaven stands at attention.

The Wake-Up Call

I'll never forget the day I caught myself praying a safe prayer. You know the one—"Lord, just help me make it through..." *Just?* Help me just make it? When did I start asking God for crumbs and calling it faith?

I closed my eyes to pray, but felt nothing. No fire. No wind. Just air. That's when the Holy Spirit gently but firmly said, "Daughter, if you don't believe what you're asking for, why should I move?"

It crushed me. But it changed me. I realized my prayers were out of alignment. My lips said "I trust You," but my heart still braced for disappointment. That day, I made a decision: if I'm going to pray, I'm going to pray like I believe God hears me. Like I believe He will move. Like I believe He is still the God of miracles, signs, and wonders—because He is. And that decision? It cracked open something in the spirit. Doors started swinging open. Resources flowed. Strategies dropped in my spirit like divine downloads. Not because I said prettier words, but because I believed.

Stop Sounding the Alarm and Start Speaking with Authority

Let's be real. Some of our prayers sound more like SOS calls than royal decrees. We beg instead of declare. We plead instead of proclaim. We sound like strangers, not daughters. But the Kingdom doesn't respond to pity. It responds to powerful belief wrapped in bold obedience. You have the authority to speak healing. You have the power to call down peace. You have the inheritance to decree overflow. You are not praying as a victim; you are praying from the position of power and inheritance. You don't have to shout for God to hear you, but you do have to believe.

Let This Be Your New Prayer Attitude

Pray as if the job is already yours, not from a place of wishing. Pray with expectation, not explanation. Pray with your hands lifted and your mouth open. Pray until you feel the shift inside of you before you see the shift around you. Pray because you know your Father loves you, not because you're trying to earn it.

Prayer Tools for Power-Filled Believers

1. Pray Scripture. Don't just pray your feelings—pray God's Word. "I am the head and not the tail." (Deut. 28:13) "No weapon formed against me shall prosper." (Isa. 54:17) "My steps are ordered by the Lord." (Ps. 37:23). Scripture is not just words in a book. It's a battle plan.

2. Pray with Vision. Don't just ask God to fix it, ask Him to reveal it. "God, what do You want me to learn in this season? What are You trying to birth through this burden?" Praying with vision brings divine clarity to your current season.

3. Pray out loud. Silence is not always golden; sometimes it's the enemy's muzzle. Say it loud. Walk the floor. Wake up the atmosphere. There is so much power in your spoken word.

4. Pray in Community. Yes, your private prayer matters. But some breakthroughs need agreement. Call your prayer warriors. Join prayer calls. Touch and agree with other believers. Storm the gates together. There is a release of power when two or more gather in His name.

Prayer to Get You Started, When You're Weary but Still Expecting

Father God, I don't want to pray like I'm not sure that You'll show up. I don't want to mumble my requests out of fear or fatigue. Help me understand that You are not afraid of boldness. You are waiting for it. So here I am, Lord, praying like a daughter who knows she's loved. Praying like I believe You are who You say You are. I release every small prayer, every doubt-soaked whisper to you. I declare: this is the day heaven hears me roar. In Jesus' name. Amen.

Reflection: Pray Like You Know Who You Are

Pray Like You Believe

You have come too far to whisper prayers rooted in fear. You have survived storms, outlasted heartbreak, and kept showing up. Now it's time to *pray like you know who you are*. You are not the woman who second-guesses every *ask* or apologizes for needing help. You are the woman God listens to. The one who speaks, and angels are dispatched. The one who dares to believe again, not because life has been perfect, but because your faith refuses to die. The same fire that carried you through the last season is now being stirred to ignite something new. God has been waiting; not for perfection, but for your faith to grow. You are not begging. You are building. Every prayer is a step forward to the breakthrough.

So, here's the call: start praying from victory, not from doubt. Speak like heaven is leaning in, because it is. Pray like the healed version of yourself, even if you are still in the process of recovering. Your words have power. Your obedience is the bridge between this moment and your next miracle. Don't just close this, wishing things would happen, *activate* it. Write down your boldest prayers. Say them out loud. Watch your faith increase and watch things change in your favor. Keep praying until the valley becomes your testimony. This is your new way of living.

Questions

1. What have your prayers sounded like lately—faith or fear?

_____
_____
_____
_____
_____
_____

Pray Like You Believe

2. Have you been praying for outcomes you secretly don't believe can happen?

   _____
   _____
   _____
   _____
   _____
   _____
   _____

3. What would shift if you started praying as if it were already done?

   _____
   _____
   _____
   _____
   _____
   _____
   _____

4. Are there areas where you've stopped praying altogether? Why?

   _____
   _____
   _____
   _____
   _____
   _____
   _____

5. What scriptures can you stand on and declare out loud this week?

6. Who can you pray with in agreement for a breakthrough?

7. What are three bold, specific prayers you will commit to praying daily for the next 21 days?

Journal Prompt: *Pray Like You Believe*

When did your prayers become filled with doubts and an unappreciated obligation? When did you start just going through the motions of prayer? When did you stop flipping tables in the spirit and start whispering around mountains that need to be moved? When did you stop praying with expectation and start praying to survive? Search your soul and ask:

Pray Like You Believe

What do I believe about prayer? Is God listening? Does He really care about my troubles? Do I believe it's just a routine, a ritual, a lifeline I clutch in desperation, or do I believe it is a weapon of mass construction, reshaping atmospheres, and unlocking destiny?

Now write this with holy honesty: *Where am I still praying small, safe prayers because I'm afraid God won't answer? Where have I been praying from memory and not from faith?*

This time, dig deeper. If I truly believed God was listening not just to my words, but to the depths of my heart, what would I pray for today? Not someday. Not when I'm stronger. Not if everything aligns. What would I ask for now, boldly, audaciously, relentlessly? Write that prayer. Write it like Heaven is leaning in. Write it like the chains are already breaking. Write it like the answer is already on its way because it is definitely on the way to you.

_____
_____
_____
_____
_____
_____
_____
_____
_____
_____
_____
_____
_____
_____

Pray Like You Believe

Prayer: To Be Prayed Aloud, with Bold Faith

Father, in the mighty name of Jesus,

I come before You not as a beggar, but as a believer. Not as a woman hoping that You will hear me, but as a daughter who knows You hear and see me. Today, I lay down the powerless prayers, the whispering prayers soaked in doubt, and I pick up the mantle of bold, unwavering belief. I come boldly to Your throne of mercy, not because I am perfect, but because Your grace says I can.

I declare with belief in my spirit and Your words in my mouth: I believe You, God. I believe You are who You say You are. I believe You still perform miracles, open wombs, restore broken families, and heal hearts that bleed in secret. I believe You still answer in fire, in whisper, in thunder, and silence. You are not limited by what limits me. And so, I refuse to shrink in my asking. I will pray like a daughter who knows her Heavenly Father is listening.

God, teach me to pray with vision, not just emotion. Please help me to trust that even when I don't see movement, there's still momentum. Cancel every lie that says my voice doesn't matter. Erase every seed of doubt that keeps me from asking boldly. Make my heart a sanctuary of faith. Let every prayer I release shake the gates of hell and bring heaven's glory down to earth.

And Lord, God, when I feel tired, when I am weary from waiting, breathe life back into my belief. Let me remember that You never sleep or slumber. You are always listening, always moving, and always making ways where there seem to be none. So today, and every day forward, I will pray like I believe that Your word is true, because I do. In Jesus' name. Amen.

LLYB Declaration
I Will Pray with The Volume of My Faith, Not The Volume of My Fear

I will no longer water down my prayers to match my doubt. I will no longer whisper to a God who commands the seas and places all the stars in the sky. I will pray like the daughter of the King that I am. My words carry weight. My voice shakes things loose. I will *Pray Like I Believe,* because I *do* believe. Belief is my weapon. I will pray with the volume of my faith, not the volume of my fear. My prayers will be fresh every morning, just like the grace and mercy of God. I will no longer treat prayer as a routine or a task on a to-do list, but as a lifeline to my Father's heart. I know I am not praying into the wind. I am praying into the ear of a faithful, loving, all-powerful God who still answers. God is not punishing me with silence. Sometimes He is growing my voice in the waiting, but even in that quiet, I will not retreat. I will rise. I will ask boldly. I will believe again. I will not be discouraged when circumstances have not changed quickly after I pray. I will be empowered by who God is. He has not changed. His Word has not changed. His promises have not expired. Maybe, just maybe, God is waiting for *me* to pray like I believe it is already done. I will pray again, but this time, from a stance that I am already healed. I will pray with gratitude that my loved ones are already healed and that my family is reconciled. I will pray from my I-know-Who-I-belong-to self. I will not serve a transactional God in my mind and then expect relational power in my life. My prayers will come from a place of deep surrender and unshakable faith. This isn't just a Power Move, it's my permission slip to pray without limits. I was born to believe and agree with heaven.

THE FINAL PAGE—NEVER THE END

"She remembered who she was, and the rising became non-negotiable." — Loretta McNary

If you're here, reading these words, I want you to know I see you. I've been you. I *am* you, a woman carrying both ache and ambition. One who has loved deeply, lost deeply, and still dared to rise.

This book was never just about words it was about you stepping fully into your light. It was about giving you permission to stop asking for permission. To stop shrinking so others feel comfortable. To stop pretending you're okay when you're unraveling inside.

I wrote these pages in the quiet between my own heartbreak and healing in the sacred stillness after life flipped everything upside down.

I was healing from physical trauma, adjusting to a new normal with titanium rods and screws holding my bones together, while still showing up to host my show from the corner of my living room; pain hidden, walker off camera.

But through that pain, something divine was being born. This book. This movement. This message: *"Live Like You Believe."*

Now you've made it to the last page. But *don't close this book too quickly.*

Come back often. Let these pages be your rhythm. Your refuge. Your reminder. Some chapters will hit differently on new days. Let them. That's the beauty of becoming. Each version of you will see something the last one didn't. Because this isn't just a story - it's a *mirror*. A map. A mantle. You weren't called to do it all alone. You don't have to carry everything. There is power in giving. But there is beauty in receiving, too.

I know it can be hard to ask for help, but hear me: You are not less because you need support. You are *human*. You are *holy*. You are *worthy* of the love that pours into you, too.

So, as one woman *becoming* to another, keep telling your story. Stop hiding. Let someone see your truth. Your vulnerability might give someone else the courage to speak.

Your healing could light someone else's path. And if ever you forget your power, come back here. Let these pages remind you of who you are. Return to them whenever your faith wavers or your courage dims.

This is your moment to commit to complete healing. I hope after reading "Live Like You Believe," you will allow your healing to begin, and that you will stop pretending that *barely getting by* is the same as thriving. I pray you will stop believing that *not bad* is the best that life has to offer, and that you will stop performing like the wound isn't real.

I encourage you to rip off the proverbial bandage. Call your healing what it is: holy, hard, necessary. *Live like you believe* you deserve more. *Live like you believe* you are worth the miracles. *Live like you believe* that He still has a plan, because He does. And His plan for you is so much bigger than you could ever imagine.

Tell yourself, "I will heal for real. I will stop pretending that survival is enough. I will stop wearing perfection as a mask to hide my pain. I will not apologize for my process or minimize my needs. I will heal out loud. I will rest without guilt. I will tell the truth, even when my voice shakes. I will rise; not because I am unbreakable, but because I have finally stopped hiding the places where I was broken.

I will live like I believe that God will heal the woman behind the bandage. I live with grace, sisterhood, and fierce faith!

I will live like I believe because I know this is not the end, but the beginning - it's our crescendo! The rising note that shatters glass ceilings and forces the best inside of us to shine. The soul cry that says, "I'm not shrinking anymore. I am healed. I have risen. I am leading."

Now it is time to pray like all of heaven is waiting for us, because Heaven is waiting for us to Heal, to Rise, and to Lead. I dare you to embrace all 10 Power Moves each day, and watch mountains move. We will still have storms, challenges, and trials, but the peace that surpasses understanding will be our prize through it all. And this will keep us seeking God and finding Him every time. When we find Him, we will find and connect with the best version of us. And this version will always *live like we believe.*

About Loretta

Loretta McNary is a global media personality, an award-winning transformational speaker, author, and philanthropist who has dedicated her life to empowering others to rise, heal, and lead with purpose. As the host and executive producer of *The Loretta McNary Show, Mornings with Loretta,* and *Women Leading by Faith,* she has captivated and inspired audiences for over two decades through powerful interviews and impactful storytelling.

Loretta is the founder and CEO of *Women On the Move Reimagined*, a monthly networking luncheon that connects and equips women entrepreneurs, corporate professionals, and visionaries who crave meaningful community and unstoppable growth. She is also the founder of *Pink Eagles Inc.,* a nonprofit leadership development organization for girls designed to foster confidence, purpose, and potential in the next generation of changemakers.

As the CEO of McNary Media Network and creator of the *Live Like You Believe Movement,* Loretta continues to uplift and activate individuals through books, coaching, and storytelling. But her most cherished role is being the proud mother of five amazing sons; Brandon, Marshall, Nicholas, Spencer and Jacob. Through every season, Loretta embodies what she teaches: faith over fear, gratitude through storms, and boldness without apology.

Other Books by Loretta

"Faith for the Next Step: 52 Messages to Inspire and Encourage"

This empowering devotional offers the reader 52 soul-strengthening messages—one for each week of the year. Designed for women navigating change, healing, or growth, Loretta delivers wisdom-filled encouragement and practical steps rooted in scripture, resilience, and divine timing. This book is for the woman who knows her next step requires both courage and faith, and refuses to shrink.

"Hope for the Next Step: 365 Days of Inspiration & Encouragement"

Every day is a new opportunity to choose hope. This 365-day devotional features daily words of inspiration to reset your mindset, lift your heart, and align your spirit with joy, peace, and God's promises. A perfect companion for women seeking consistent encouragement and spiritual clarity as they journey through all of life's seasons.

CONNECT WITH LORETTA

Loretta would love to hear from you! Stay connected with her community, upcoming events, books, and live appearances by visiting her website or following her on social media. Whether you're stepping into a new season, launching something bold, or simply looking for connection, you don't have to do it alone. Join our global community at www.LiveLikeYouBelieve.net

Website: www.LorettaMcNary.com

YouTube: Loretta McNary Show

Facebook: Loretta McNary Show

Instagram: @LorettaMcNaryShow

www.Twitter.com/LorettaMcNary

www.linkedin.com/in/lorettamcnary

Podcast: **Live Like You Believe**
Coming Soon

Want to share how this book impacted you?
Use the hashtag **#LiveLikeYouBelieve**
tag **@LorettaMcNaryShow**

Let's fill the world with stories of women *becoming*. Your story could inspire someone else's next step! Even on our hardest days, even in the quiet valleys, even when no one else sees us, God does. I do.
And now, so do you.

> *"She remembered who she was and the rising became non-negotiable."*
>
> LORETTA MCNARY

www.ingramcontent.com/pod-product-compliance
Lightning Source LLC
Chambersburg PA
CBHW051952290426
44110CB00015B/2214